THE ENCYCLOPEDIA OF
ROOTICAL FOLKLORE

THE **ENCYCLOPEDIA** OF **ROOTICAL FOLKLORE**

PLANT TALES FROM AFRICA AND THE DIASPORA

NATTY MARK SAMUELS

with collage illustrations by
Nancey B. Price

SCORCHED EARTH PRESS
Saxtons River, VT

Distributed to trade in the US by Microcosm Publishing and in the UK by Turnaround Publishing Services.

Special discounts are available for bulk purchases by organizations and institutions. Please email orders@scorchedearthpress.com for more information.

ISBN 978-1-96192-405-5

Cover artwork: "Trifolium" © Bienvenue Fotso / African Art Beats
Collage illustrations on unnumbered pages © 2023 Nancey B. Price
Book design by Maya Gupta & Rebecca LeGates

The excerpt from "The Humps" on p. xiii is from *The Tales of Amadou Koumba* by Birago Diop, translated by Dorothy S. Blair. Copyright © 1966 by Oxford University Press.

The poem "Souffles" on p. xiv is from *Leurres et Lueurs*, copyright © 1960 by Birago Diop.

"The Baobab Monologue" was previously published in the chapbook, *The Birago Diop Trilogy*, by Reamsworth Publishing, © Natty Mark Samuels, 2021.

"Chaney Root Chant," "Tale of Chili Pepper," "Tale of Dates," "Tale of a Fig Grove," "Tale of Guava," "Tale of Sorrel," "Tale of Lemongrass," "The Mango Juggler" (as "Tale of Mangifera"), "Tale of a Pea Harvest," "Tale of a Rose," "Tale of Rose Apple," "Like Sly and Robbie," and "Tale of Tamarind" were released as digital downloads collectively titled *The Papine Tales* by Wisemind Publications, © Natty Mark Samuels, 2022.

LCCN 2023945734 | ISBN 9781961924055

This book is published by Scorched Earth Press: books for beyond the end of the world. Buy it somewhere that's not Amazon.

Scorched Earth Press
P.O. Box 294
Saxtons River, VT 05154
www.scorchedearthpress.com
thehumans@scorchedearthpress.com

Printed in the USA by Versa.

To Harold Courlander
and Isidore Okpewho

Contents

Editor's Note

Plants have roots; so do people. Rootical Folklore is about the intertwining of human and plant roots in Africa and the African Diaspora. Plants and people, when they grow with one another through the centuries, make stories —like the ones collected in the volume you are holding.

Natty Mark Samuels has shaped these stories in many different ways. Some emerge as songs, some as call-and-response chants, some as haiku, some as dialogues, and some as prose fiction. Together, these different genres give a sense of the depth and richness of the soils in which these tales' roots lie.

"Diaspora" is itself a botanical word, Greek for "a scattering of seeds." In tracing the travels of seeds, Rootical Folklore represents a wide-angle vision of African Diaspora. Samuels tells how date fruits journeyed across Sudan and who brought arrowroot on a canoe from Venezuela. There's a place here for the lore of the Guaraní and of the amaMpondo.

Some of the the plant protagonists of these pieces, such as peanuts and oranges, may be daily companions for most of us; others, like jatoba and umabophe, will probably need some introduction. We have written a brief botanical and historical description of each plant, for you to read or skip as you like. Either way, we hope that setting science and story side by side in this Encyclopedia will help show the limitations of a knowledge that comes only from the former. You can use Wikipedia to learn what a plant is, but only through stories can you find out who they are.

Samuels's tales don't just help us come to know plants; they show plants helping us come to know ourselves. A baobab tree provides an overview of West African folklore ("The Baobab Monologue"), while African lettuce becomes a point of contact with the Nigerian painter Prince Twins Seven Seven ("I Will Bring You African Lettuce"). A trumpet tree duets the Crucian cariso singer Mama Leona Watson and takes part in the triumphal procession of Queen Idia of Benin, all in a single instant. In *The Encyclopedia of Rootical Folklore*, plants are how African culture takes root in the present, with "ancestors threading in and out."

Acknowledgements

Saluting Junie James, a.k.a. Sista Junie, who I call Great Elder—founder/director of ACKHI, based in Oxford—for assistance with this book in its embryonic stage. Long-time cultural activist and the first and most consistent supporter of African School. The other two original supporters are Christine Chambers, the first publicist, and Pat Green, both resident in Oxford.

In putting this encyclopedia together, I have to acknowledge Sharon Barcan Elswit. Her two books, *The Caribbean Story Finder* and *The Latin American Story Finder,* have been indispensable to this endeavor, making past research and present writing an easier task.

An eternal thanksgiving to Petra Bakewell-Stone, ethnobotanist, for her support of the folklore section of the African School Library.

And the same length of gratitude to Jacqueline Forrester (Working Men's College) and Elli Dimaki (Chelsea Physic Garden), London; Anita Shervington (BLAST), Birmingham; Ras Flako (Wisemind Publications), Jamaica; Marco Fregnan, (Reggaediscography), Italy; Babacar M'Baye (Kent State University); University of Portsmouth; Cambridge University Botanic Garden; Sheffield Botanical Garden;

The *Sentinel* (St. Kitts and Nevis); Dan Glazebrook (Oxford Spires Academy); Michelle Johnson (Chilworth House Upper School); Fusion Arts; Oxford Science Festival; Jacqui Gitau (African Families UK); Oxford University Botanic Garden; C.D.I. (Community Development Initiative); and Blackbird Leys Library, Oxford, for their ongoing support of African Studies through African School, offering more opportunities to share the oral traditions. Special thank you to Anita Shervington, Jacqueline Forrester, Marco Fregnan, and Dane Comerford, the greatest supporters of Rootical Folklore.

Preface

Rootical Folklore began with a tamarind tree. You could say that this encyclopedia is a branch of that tree. But which tamarind do I speak of? The one that is mentioned in "The Humps," the first story in *The Tales of Amadou Koumba,* by the Senegalese polymath Birago Diop.

> *Momor and Koumba had never offended the spirits, nor hurt them by either actions or words; so they could rest beneath the shade of the tamarind without fearing either visit or vengeance from the evil spirits.*

It's this tamarind, abode of ancestral spirits, alongside the paramountcy given to the oral traditions by African philosophers of the early 20th century such as Stefano Kaoze (Congo) and John Mbuti (Kenya), that led me into the research of African and Caribbean folklore through flora: the spiritual significance of plants.

As each believer, through whatever text or gatherings, finds their way to God, so it is with ancestral recognition. The research and my subsequent writings—the content of this book—have given me a deeper insight into African spirituality before the coming of what are called "organized religions" and have offered me another reason to celebrate the continent where my roots lie. When I go to the river now, as well as giving thanks for Creation, I pour a libation of lemon water, my favorite drink, to

Yemoja and Oshun, two of the Yoruba orishas (deities) associated with rivers. This is the significance behind the chant in "The Baobab Monologue":

Whispering, listening,
Weaving of whispering,
Ancestors threading in and out.

If we look at the Oromo of Ethiopia, whether they're Muslim or Christian, they still gather to give thanks at the annual Irreechaa Festival; the same interreligious attendance is seen at the Osogbo-Osun Festival in Nigeria. Both of these events happen by bodies of water: a lake and a river.

With his *Tales of Amadou Koumba*, published in 1947, the aforementioned Diop ushered in the postwar publication of African folktales. As well as that collection of tales, Diop gave us the poem "Souffles," or "Breaths." For me, it's one of two great short poems of ancestral celebration through nature; the other is "The Negro Speaks of Rivers," by Langston Hughes. "Souffles" is invigorating, sending you again to the river or forest, or your back garden when it is quiet. It must be pure delight to read it in its French original.

Listen in the wind
To the sigh of the bush:
This is the ancestors breathing.

Using the Yellow Cedar or Yellow Trumpet Tree, the national tree of the U.S. Virgin Islands, I celebrate a more recent ancestor, Leona Watson, the iconic figure of Cariso music; she sang the songs first sung by the enslaved on

St. Croix: "Come, Yellow Trumpet Tree, play the Cariso Concerto for me. And let the lead trumpeter play, on and on, the Mama Leona Eulogy." Another recent ancestress, celebrated in "The Mango Juggler," is the Jamaican folklorist and performer Louise Bennet, a.k.a. Miss Lou.

> *The Mango Juggler always wore yellow and green and only appeared on one day of the year: September 7th, the birthday of Miss Lou. Where he came from, no one knows and where he went to after the performance, we were equally ignorant. He came, performed, and went.*

So why "Rootical"? From the first syllable, with its obvious connection to flora, to the meaning of rootical: the beginning or root of an idea. This encyclopedia, then, is part of the roots of a long-term celebration of African and Caribbean orality through plants. Rootical Folklore, because I've been digging deeper into the wider Caribbean region, encountering characters such as Tata Duende, forest guardian in Belizean orality, who has a root in Mayan culture. The silk cotton tree was sacred to the Maya, as the cypress was to the Aztec. It's taken me into the so-called Colombian Exchange, which brought yam and ackee to the Caribbean, cassava and avocado to Africa: the root of plant migrations. And "rootical" is a term of long-time use in the Diaspora, especially amongst Rasta and lovers of roots reggae, meaning something authentic, real, from the roots. Like the Sankofa bird, I go forward by looking backwards: by generating contemporary interest in ancient orality.

I see a continuation of the ancient reverence in contemporary diasporic projects, such as the Soul Fire (New York), SUSU (Vermont) and Sankofa (Philadelphia) Community Farms. For example, an excerpt from the Soul Fire website says, "With deep reverence for the land and wisdom of our ancestors, we work to reclaim our collective right to belong to the earth and to have agency in the food system." Within the SUSU statement, we read, "SUSU commUNITY Farm creates health equity by offering culturally relevant spaces that center earth based and Afro-Indigenous health and healing traditions as well as reclaiming and centering the wisdom, stories, and legacies of our ancestors." And the Sankofa site has this invitational paragraph: "As you walk through the African Diaspora Garden towards the river-side corner of Sankofa Farm at Bartram's Garden, you will pass towering sorghum, flowering sesame, okra, cotton, black-eyed peas, climbing gourds and luffa. Many of the farms that produce seed offered in this catalog are focused on growing crops connected to the experience of Africans in America. This collection includes many crops that either originated in Africa, or that became important staples in the new world."

This encyclopedia, then, is like a textual affirmation of these community farms. Whether in Africa or whatever part of the Diaspora, we pay homage to our ancestry. Before knowledge of planting and plant medicine, there was reverence, generating the spiritual significance of the flora. Before utility, there was sanctity. With reverence came protection. Some of the sacred groves of Africa have become hubs for biodiversity research, such as the Modjadji Cycad Reserve, within the domain of the Mojajdi Rain Queens of South Africa. You can still see prehistoric cycads, said to have been food of the dinosaurs, due to the care of this lineage of female monarchs.

This theme of reverence and protection echoed throughout the life of Wangari Maathai, the Kenyan environmental activist. As a child, gathering firewood with her mother, she was told, "Don't pick any dry wood out of the fig tree, or even around it....We don't use it. We don't cut it. We don't burn it." That lesson permeated her learning, fueling her later activism. In a statement from later years, she said, "The trees also prevented soil erosion, and when this traditional wisdom was no longer taught, when the idea of the holiness of trees and the biodiversity of the environment was lost, the people suffered..."

A fig tree grove stands paramount in the Creation story of the Kikuyu, the people Maathai came from. Across the other side of the continent, in traditional Ashanti belief, Thursday was seen as the day of Creation, so this was a rest day, when the land wasn't worked and nothing was taken from it. To break this ruling was a major crime in the Ashanti society of Ghana. Even with the coming of agriculture, there was still a level of sanctity; reverence continued, as we saw in that paragraph from "The Humps."

Reverence permeates this book. One of the pieces, the chant called Lady Papaya—there's a snippet below—recognises the Candomblé religion, practised in Brazil, which has its roots in Yoruba (Nigeria), Fon (Benin) and Bantu (Central, East and Southern Africa) beliefs.

Man of Bahia,
With a gift for orisha,
Kneeling there at the shrine.

As well as in Candomblé and its derivative Umbanda in Brazil, you will find orishas (Yoruba deities) central to other diasporic beliefs, such as Santería / Lukumí / Regla de Ocha in Cuba. For example, Eshu, orisha of gateways, roads and messages, has his counterpart Exu in Candomblé and Elegua in Santería; in Vodou (Haiti) and 21 Divisions (Dominican Republic), he is called Papa Legba. Each orisha has flora associated with them as offerings, herbal bath ingredients, or talismans; guava is one of the plants associated with Eshu.

Some orishas are primordial, such as Orunmila, deity of wisdom and divination; others are deified ancestors, like Shango, orisha of thunder and lightning; but whether you venerate them in Africa or the Americas, there is a commonality of offerings.

Turning to my concept of this book as an encyclopedia: the jali or griot of the Mande peoples of West Africa is an oral encyclopedia, expert in the knowledge of one subject: his people. This is manifested in many aspects, for as well as storyteller and musician, he was also spokesman, historian, genealogist, tutor, envoy, and leader of the court ensemble. The contemporary figures Toumani Diabaté, player of the kora, and Bassekou Kouyate, player of the ngoni, both born in Mali, come from acclaimed jali lineages.

I've created two diasporic figures, Jah Folk and Mama Solace, as contemporary storytellers; they keep alive the evening tradition of gathering, learning, and laughing together that I call the "Moonlit Classroom." Jah Folk, who first appears as the mouthpiece of Rootical Folklore in The Papine Tales, is based in Kingston; Mama Solace, being spirit as well as flesh, is omnipresent. As urban figures of the present, they speak of issues such as gang warfare, domestic violence, mental illness and so on; after all, these are folktales. Because Jah Folk is a folk-lorist and historian, as well as a storyteller, he's regularly invited to teach at the local high school and university. Mama Solace is mentor to many, community champion to all. She doesn't need to go anywhere, as everyone comes to her. She is a composite of all the great female leaders of the orisha temples: she is a reflection of Nana Buruku, primordial mother.

The Moonlit Classroom is how stories like the ones told here become part of people's lives. During the tradi-tional gatherings around the evening fire—now largely disappearing—when stories would be told, children would first learn the lessons of life such as respect for the elders, abhorrence of greed, the cultivation of generosity and so on; and adults would be reminded of them. The retention of the lessons in the tales would be helped by chants or songs, the main form of audience participation in the Moonlit Classroom. Here is a snippet of chant from "One Little Ackee," inspired by a Jamaican tale about the consequences of greed, when a girl with a sackful of ackees refuses to give one to the spirit of the river for safe passage across.

> *Higher and higher,*
> *Rising of water,*
> *Just the one little ackee.*

In conclusion, as I've said before, "I believe a collection of folktales carries a route to wisdom and redemptive potential, as the Bible, Koran or any religious text." Spinach features in a story about revenge; Kola nut, in a reminder of respect to the elders; Pumpkin, in one concerning karma; Coconut, in a tale about rational thinking and so on. As well as the lessons of life, plants feature as sources of rescue and salvation; in Creation stories; residence of the guardians; sacred instruments; location of spirits and so on. So if we learn from the fauna—from Anansi (spider), Mbe (tortoise) and Sungura (hare)—we can learn from the flora also: from Ackee, Plantain and Calabash.

There's an Ashanti story (with Yoruba and Igbo versions, featuring the tortoises Mbe and Ajapa respec-tively) about the celebrated arachnid, Anansi, collecting all the local wisdom and depositing it in a calabash on his back. So in conclusion, here's a poem, "Bob Marley Calabash," about a man I think of as wise, though he

passed on at thirty-six; I imagine him in childhood days
with his friend Bunny Wailer, enjoying the beauty of the
Moonlit Classroom.

> *I see you, Bob Marley,*
> *Learning through Anansi*
> *Alongside Bunny,*
> *Wrapped in the magic of Grandmother.*
> *Trickery with yams,*
> *Pea harvest theft,*
> *Invention of sorrel,*
> *The calabash of wisdom.*
> *Icon of melody,*
> *Scooping coconut jelly,*
> *Childhood revelry,*
> *Basking in the warmth of the Elder.*

ACACIA

m(g)unga, *Vachellia nilotica* syn.
Acacia arabica, gonakié, gum
arabic tree, nebneb

Acacias grow all over the world and come in many different shapes and sizes. They are the defining genus of the Sahel, the ecoregion that separates North Africa from the Sahara, and the umbrella thorn acacia is perhaps the savanna's most iconic tree.

V. nilotica, one of several species known as the gum arabic tree, is a thorny tree with sunny yellow pom-poms for flowers and seeds resembling foot-long peas—no accident, since acacias are in fact legumes. The tree's hard wood was valued for boatbuilding in ancient Egypt, where it grew in groves near temples and was linked with the god Osiris. Blooming acacias are depicted in tomb paintings from the 20th century BCE, alongside the same bird species that love to perch in its branches even today. Much later, in Senegal, the French clearcut vast forests of *V. nilotica* to fuel their steamboats' colonial voyages upriver—to the point that they altered the country's climate and had to create forest reserves for the tree.

Many parts of the plant may be made into medicine; the Swahili, amongst others, use acacia leaf tea to soothe a sore throat. The Swahili hero and poet Fumo Liyongo mentioned in this piece, wrote a love song in which he likens a lady's eyebrows to acacia branches.

Acacia features in the creation story of the Bamana of Mali. (See also SHEA.) It can offered to Obatala, *orisha*—Yoruba divinity—of human creation.

1

2

The Acacia Guide

Don't worry, little one, I will not frighten you: I'm not a generator of fear. I know the rest of the clan have a bad name, the worst of all names, but I am not a channel to harm, for I am Shuluwele.

I hear that cough of yours is getting worse and I know the famous storyteller is visiting this evening, so you won't be wanting his narrative interspersed with your utterances! Imagine, him in full flow, maybe talking of the great Liyongo—and there's you, spitter-spattering all over the place! So come, let's make a visit to Acacia and ask her a sample of remedy. She's usually a generous soul, offering what she has. We'll ask her for a few leaves, just enough to make a brew to ease that pain in your throat. Come, little one, I'll be your guide to the Bountiful One.

Yes, little sufferer, I am of the Shetani Clan, those highly skilled in evil, but I am just a signposter, pointing the way to relief. I'm just a collector of medicine: I am Shuluwele.

In the folklore of the Swahili and other peoples of the wider East African region, the shetani are devilish spirits—their name is cognate with "Satan." The Makonde people resident in that region, renowned for their sculpting, depict these characters in their carving. Shetani also appear in the paintings of Makonde artist George Lilanga.

ACKEE

isin, ewe ochin, seso vegetal, pommier finsam, castanheiro-de-áfrica, *Blighia sapida*

Ackee is an evergreen tree native to West Africa, related to lychee and longan. Its name comes from Twi, a language of Ghana. Ackee seeds arrived in Jamaica on a slave ship in the eighteenth century and quickly naturalized in the lowlands there; today, it is Jamaica's national fruit, celebrated in festivals and place names.

The yellow flesh of the ackee fruit, when ripe, is edible, with an almost tofu-like consistency and an eggy taste. It is cooked in savory dishes with leafy vegetables or, in the classic Jamaican dish, paired with saltfish—the salt cod once traded by New Englanders for Caribbean molasses. But the seeds and waxy red rind of the ackee, and the flesh too of the unripe fruit, are poisonous, even deadly. So one must wait to pick ackee until the rind splits open, or "smiles," revealing the three fleshy arils, each tipped with a large glossy seed.

The tree's genus, *Blighia*, is named after William Bligh, the infamous captain of the *Bounty*, the main objective of whose sea voyages was to engage in bioprospecting on behalf of English botanical impresario Joseph Banks. To that end, Bligh took seeds of BREADFRUIT from Tahiti to Jamaica (mutiny notwithstanding)—and took seeds of ackee, in turn, from Jamaica to London's Kew Gardens.

In the Afro-Cuban religion of Lukumí or Santería, ackee is one of the trees of the orisha Obatala, and its fruit may be used to cure insanity.

One Little Ackee

There is a tale from Jamaica about greed and learning the hard way, in which two girls out collecting ackee come to a dry river. The spirit of the river asks for one ackee from each girl in exchange for letting them pass through safely. One of the girls gives one straight away; the other refuses. So he brings water in. And at her continued refusal of the admonitions of friend and spirit, water rises, and the inevitable happens. I imagine the spirit of the river chanting for his fruit of appeasement:

> Only one, only one,
> Throw it in, greedy girl,
> Just the one little ackee.

> Higher and higher,
> Rising of water,
> Just the one little ackee.

> Up to your eyeball,
> Won't last till nightfall,
> Just the one little ackee.

> Only one, only one,
> Throw it in, greedy girl,
> Just the one little ackee.

AFRICAN LETTUCE

wonto, efo yanrin, ugu, dadedru, *Launaea taraxacifolia,* katapka

At one time, most towns in Yorubaland had sacred groves, where no one could fell trees or hunt. Now, few such groves remain, but one that does is the grove by the river Osun. In it grow many plants dear to Oshun, the orisha of freshwater and fertility who gives the river its name; African lettuce is among them. A woman who wishes to conceive will bring a dish of cooked African lettuce to the grove, to the statue of Oshun's delegate Olomoyoyo, or offer it directly to the orisha herself. The plant may also be used as part of a prayer for rainfall, which Oshun controls.

African lettuce is indeed a close relative of domesticated lettuce, with rough deeply lobed leaves and starry yellow flowers resembling tiny dandelions. It grows throughout the African tropics, the kind of unprepossessing plant outsiders tend to overlook, though in Benin alone there are at least nine different vernacular names for it. Like the prickly lettuces of temperate zones, African lettuce is tough, able to withstand drought and lean soil. It often appears spontaneously in the garden, and many welcome its presence there or gather it from the wild. In some regions, African lettuce or its East African sibling *L. cornuta* are among the most widely consumed vegetables. The nutritious leaves are eaten fresh or cooked in soup, and the leaves, seeds, and milky sap all have a wide range of therapeutic virtues.

I Shall Bring You African Lettuce

If I could, Lady of the River, I would take the same steps as Prince Seven Seven, past the places of worship and the sculpture of benediction, making my way to you. Who better to guide me through the sacred grove that carries your name?

Did you ever see his painting called *Arugba Osun*? I like the pattern on the cloth covering the calabash, reminiscent of rows of cowrie shells. The calabash of offerings to you. You, sentinel of the river, watcher over heron and kingfisher, toad and tilapia: we know you cast your eye over us also.

Tell me, what did Prince bring to you? Honey? Pumpkin? Spinach? When I come to you, Goddess Oshun, I shall bring you African Lettuce.

An annual festival, Osun-Oshogbo, is held in honor of the orisha Os(h)un in the sacred grove alongside the Osun River in Nigeria. For more on Prince Seven Seven, see ALLIGATOR PEPPER

ALFALFA

lucerne, *Medicago sativa,* barsim

Alfalfa is a clover relative with trifoliate leaves and purple flowers. It has been grown as a forage crop in what is now Iran since before recorded history (the name "alfalfa" comes from an Old Iranian word meaning "horse food") and Persians introduced the plant to Greece in antiquity. During the Middle Ages, Europe gave up growing plants for fodder, but alfalfa cultivation continued in Northern Africa. From there, it was reintroduced to Spain during the Muslim conquest, along with irrigation systems—qanats and acequias—that satisfied the plant's high water needs. Today, drought threatens alfalfa production in many parts of the world, but in northern New Mexico, community-managed acequias still water alfalfa fields, via a hybrid of Andalusian and Pueblo Indian technologies.

Like clover and most members of the legume family, alfalfa partners with bacteria living in its roots to turn nitrogen from the air into plant proteins. This stored nitrogen improves the soil and makes the plant nutritious for livestock. Alfalfa is especially valuable because it is a perennial and can extend its nitrogen-fixing roots as far as thirty feet into the ground. George Washington Carver, whose study of legumes was by no means limited to peanuts, hailed alfalfa as the "king of all fodder plants" after trialing it in his research fields.

Alfalfa needs bees for pollination, and a special species of bee has been introduced to North America from Europe which pollinates alfalfa more efficiently. The plant serves as a nursery for many insects, including the edible *chapulines.*

Alfalfa Soliloquy

And there we were, sitting in the presence of Mama Solace under the famous mango tree. Celebrating with Danilo, who'd just finished his mechanics apprenticeship. Relishing barbecued magic washed down with coconut water. People came and went, voicing congratulations, embracing, touching fists, bringing laughter. That was one of the things that endeared her to us. She never ate flesh, but was happy to barbecue meat and fry fish for her visitors. She never drank, either, but would allow the consumption of sugarcane liquor, because respect empowered the interaction of all who entered her compound: I never saw drunkenness there.

Reminding us always to give thanks when we touch achievement, she spoke of Ogun, orisha of iron, and an item of flora associated with him. So we gave thanks to the Creator; to the parents of Danilo; to his mentor; and to the deity of metal with a poem from her legendary box.

> I'm one of small seed,
> And when you take what you need,
> Take a portion to Ogun.
> I come in a cluster
> Used daily for fodder,

Take a portion to Ogun.
Whatever you do with me,
Healing or culinary,
I am Alfalfa;
I'm one to offer—
Take a portion to Ogun.

Mama Solace, like Jah Folk, is a character I'm using to introduce Rootical Folklore, particularly West African spirituality from before the coming of Christianity and Islam, with a focus on the Orisha (Yoruba) and Vodun (Benin) religions and their diasporic derivatives, such as Santería (Cuba), Vodou (Haiti) and Shango (Trinidad), in the Americas and elsewhere. Whereas Jah Folk is flesh, sometimes Mama Solace comes as spirit: omnipresent. She has the herbal knowledge of Loko, loa (spirit) of plants and healing, and the nurturing skills of Yemoja, orisha (deity) of motherhood and the sea. Mama Solace is mentor to many, community champion of all, empowered by her love of flora and by its spiritual significance. People gather round the mango tree in her compound as she dips into her legendary box of reflections, dispensing wisdom.

ALLIGATOR PEPPER

ose oji, ataare, *Aframomum melegueta* or *danielii,* chitta

The alligator pepper plant, a cousin of ginger and a more distant relative of BANANA and HELICONIA, loves shade, growing in wet ground under the cover of rainforest trees and in cocoa plantations. The "pepper" itself is not a tender fruit like a capsicum, but a pod containing pungent seeds, just like black cardamom, a close relative. The name "alligator pepper" refers to the pods of either *A. danielii* or *A. melegueta.* Seeds of the latter are called "grains of paradise"—a spice now known in the West chiefly to cocktail fans, but so popular in the sixteenth century that the English dubbed the area of West Africa where they sourced the seeds "The Grain Coast." *A. melegueta* is also the namesake of the kind of CHILI PEPPER that Afro-Brazilians used in the New World to replace their familiar spice: *pimenta-malagueta.*

Among the Yoruba and Igbo, the seeds or "grains" of alligator pepper are items of courtesy and ceremony, as is kola nut, also mentioned in this piece. In a practice that continues not only in Africa but in the Aukan Maroon community of Suriname, the chewed grains are rubbed on an infant's head to aid the proper development of their skull.

In Yoruba religion, alligator pepper is associated with the orisha Ogun, as are the other plants chanted in this piece.

The Alligator Pepper Duet

Imagine if you were given the opportunity to converse with your favorite artists, past and present. Amongst those I'd like to speak with are two from Nigeria: Uche Okeke of the Igbo and Prince Seven Seven from the Yoruba. Speaking of their art—influenced by their oral traditions—I'd like to talk with each of them about alligator pepper in their respective cultures:

I

Talk with me of alligator pepper, Uche Okeke, chant "ose oji" for me.

I hear it is the spice of the newborn. So on that day, during those moments of dedication and prayer, alongside kola nut, is there any flora higher? For example, on those days for your four children—Salma, Ijeoma, Chuma, and Chinedu—was ose oji paramount?

I was wondering, great elder, if on all the bodies and walls your mother painted, in the times of Uli embellishment, did she ever depict this West African plant? Can it be seen in your Oja Suite? Did it appear on any of the canvases of the students at Nsukka?

So many questions, elder, but we can discuss them later or another time: I hope there'll be another time. For now, can we return to the original point? Please talk me through the significance of the naming ceremony and alligator pepper's importance to it.

II

I keep going back to it, that piece in purple, red, yellow, and green. Yes, Prince Seven Seven, I keep going back to that painting, whose title begins with the words "Worshiping Ogun." The guns, vertical, stand like props to the shrine, and in the back, we see part of a farm, offering evidence of more metal usage: the farmer needs a blade for both the hoe and machete. So in Africa or the Americas, among the offerings to Ogun is the West African spice.

Pomegranate and Grape,
Garlic and Banana,
Alongside Alligator Pepper.

And does the painting portray the Olojo Festival, when the Ooni went to Okemogun Shrine? And the whole of Ife and beyond came to say thank you, for we all interact with iron. Hairdresser, mechanic, pilot, taxi driver, cook, hunter, farmer, and so on follow the Ooni, an entourage of celebration, proceeding to the place of gratitude. In the spiritual heartland of the Yoruba, the people follow their leader, giving thanks to the orisha of metal, deity of everyday necessity.

<blockquote>
Watermelon and Hawthorn,
Plantain and Alfalfa,
Alongside Alligator Pepper.
</blockquote>

Ife is the spiritual heartland of the Yoruba. Uche Okeke (Igbo) and Prince Seven Seven (Yoruba), are two of the giants of modern art. Uli is a traditional art form—of wall and body decoration—practiced by women. The mother of Uche Okeke was an Uli artist. He took it from its original setting, generating Ulism, when he taught at Nsukka University in Igboland. Ooni is the traditional title for the ruler of Ife, the spiritual heartland of the Yoruba, where they believe humanity began. He presides at the Olojo Festival, an annual thanksgiving to Ogun, orisha (deity) of iron. All the flora mentioned are associated with Ogun.

15

ALOE

sabr, sábila, sentebibu, babosa, *Aloe vera* syn. *barbadensis*, enkaka

His first time across the Atlantic, Columbus believed he'd discovered a trove of aloe, a plant that in its native Africa and Arabia had been used as a medicine and cosmetic for thousands of years (including, reputedly, in Cleopatra's beauty regimen.) He was wrong: what he'd found was agave, similar in appearance but unrelated and lacking the analgesic gel in its succulent leaves. Aloe would soon reach the New World with the conquistadors, though, spreading quickly to the Caribbean islands and then throughout the tropics. (Its species name derives from Linnaeus's mistaken belief that the plant originated in Barbados.)

It was not the first time someone had colonized for aloe.

Alexander the Great supposedly sent his armies to the remote Indian Ocean isle of Socotra to cultivate its endemic aloe species; aloe featured in the ancient Greek remedy *hiera pikra*, "holy bitters," which supposedly originated in the temples of Asklepios, god of healing. In the 17th century, the Dutch established aloe plantations on Aruba, Bonaire, and Curaçao to keep Europe supplied with aloe-containing purgative "dinner pills."

Aloe is given as an offering to Yemoja, Mother of Waters, orisha of motherhood and the sea: like her, aloe is cool and gentle. This piece alludes to a practice of residents of Saint Martin, who hang aloe on their doorways as a domestic talisman.

Aloe Vera Chant

Aloe Vera,
I beg you, come nearer,
Let me place you above the door.
Don't need no skin care
Or the medicinal—
I require a talisman.
Let me place you above the door.

ARROWROOT

arrurruz, *Maranta arundinacea*, hulankeeriya, uraró, obedience plant

The sibling of a popular house-plant, *Maranta leuconeura* or prayer plant, arrowroot has obvious ornamental value, with lovely white flowers and large ovate leaves. Less obvious is how to make food from its rhizomes. They must be washed, cleaned of their papery scales, re-washed, pounded, soaked, sieved, and the resultant starch dried in the sun.

Yet inhabitants of Panama and northern South America discovered how to cultivate the arrowroot plant for food between seven and ten thousand years ago, along with lerén, squash, and CALABASH. Almost as long ago, the Caribbean Arawak people adopted the plant as a staple. The name "arrowroot" itself likely has nothing to do with arrows, but is a borrowing from the Arawak language.

Arrowroot is often sold as a cornstarch substitute. It can also serve as an alternative to wheat flour, made into madungo bakes (dumplings) or arrowroot cookies, beloved from St. Martin to the Philippines.

"Mama Maranta" celebrates the Arrowroot Festival of St. Martin, held every year in February.

Mama Maranta

I guess you came with Cassava, Arrowroot; on a canoe from Venezuela, Arrowroot; propelled by the Arawak across the Caribbean Sea. Onward from Trinidad along the Antillean chain, the prettiest necklace sea or ocean has ever worn.

Ahhh, it must be heartening for you to have an adopted country hold a festival in your name. Not just a one-off, no, no: an annual honoring. Picking and stripping, Arrowroot; washing and pounding, Arrowroot: the legendary dance of pestle and mortar.

Yes, Mama Maranta, every year in a village called Colombier, people from all over gather, giving thanks for you, enjoying arrowroot cookies.

AVOCADO

on, ahuacatl, aguacate, alligator pear, *Persea americana*, palta, mfio

Avocado trees belong to the laurel family, as the light anise scent of Mexican avocado leaves suggests, and are the only member of that family to produce an edible fruit. That fruit's thick green skin encloses a buttery flesh with a single, enormous seed at its center—an evolutionary relic of an age of giant sloths and giant armadillos that could pass such large seeds through their digestive tracts.

Avocados grow in tropical climates all over the world but were first domesticated in Mexico. For the Maya, the tree has long been a valuable member of traditional agroecosystems now known as *acahual*: orchard-gardens that grow in a fallowed *milpa* or field.

The Mexica used avocados to treat a range of ailments, from diarrhea to dandruff. In Nahuatl, the word for avocado, *ahuacatl*, is also a euphemism for testicles, early testimony to the avocado's use as an aphrodisiac.

In Jamaica, self-liberated Maroons grew the trees in the provision grounds of their communities in the mountains, since avocados will grow in highland soils too dry or steep for other crops. The leaves are used medicinally from Guyana to Nigeria, and the tree is a popular addition to streetsides in many African cities.

Ogun, orisha of metal, can be presented with avocado; purple avocados belong to Oya.

Anthem of Avocado

Walk me through, Aztec Spirit, your garden of inspired imagination, where vanilla invites one and all to a jamboree of aroma.

Who shall I dance with first—Marigold or Dahlia? In the place where chili pepper jumps, oregano rocks, I look forward to laughter with coriander.

And in the evening, can we sit in the Cinema of Green Gentleness, between pineapple and papaya, and watch the epic of the butterfly? Or sit in Iridescent Theater, while hummingbird gives a recital of poetry.

Come, Aztec Spirit, let's lean our backs against the cypress tree, drinking atole—corn, water and lime—while the garden serenades us, beginning with the Cocoa Canticles, concluding with the Anthem of Avocado.

BALSAM APPLE

Momordica balsamina, asosi, African cucumber, cerasee, ejinrin, iNtshungu, garahuni, corailee

Balsam apple is a cucumber-like vine with small warty fruits that ripen to bright orange. The leaves and the unripe fruit are widely used as vegetables in Africa, and the plant is known in both Africa and the Caribbean for its healing properties. The seeds of the fruit are enclosed in sticky scarlet arils, which are edible. Balsam apple's close relative, *M. charantia* (balsam pear, bitter gourd, karela) is similar to balsam apple, with larger and longer fruits; many common names, such as bitter melon and cerasee, are used for both species. Like balsam apple, *M. charantia* is of West African origin but is now a fixture in cuisines throughout the world, appearing in the Okinawan stir fry goya chanpuru, the Filipino dish pinakbet, in pickles or paired with coconut in India, and fried with crispy onions in Trinidad.

Balsam apple was once equally cosmopolitan. It reached Europe by 1568 as a medicinal product and was sighted growing in South Carolina in 1723, where it had likely arrived via the Middle Passage. There are many records of its use as an ornamental in early 19th-century America: Jefferson mentions its planting at Monticello, and it appeared in gardener's calendars and in a famous still life painting at the time. But in the US it has undergone a collective forgetting; few know it today, except perhaps in Florida, where it is a "nuisance to land managers."

In Yoruba religion, balsam apple is associated with stability and with Olokun, Keeper of Secrets, orisha of wealth and the deep sea. In this piece, a young person, trapped by restlessness, appeals to balsam apple for constancy.

Balsamina Chant

Come, Balsam Apple,
African Cucumber,
Generate stability.

Plant of Olokun,
That great orisha,
Deity of the sea.

Youth runs and rages
Onward to darkness,
Requesting consistency.

Redemption mission,
Rid of the shadow,
Chant Balsamina for me.

BAMBOO

Oxytenanthera abyssinica, mianzi, parun pupa, savanna bamboo

Bamboo is any of about 1,400 species of tall, fast-growing grasses. *Bambusa vulgaris* is the most common; it first grew in Southeast Asia but is now distributed throughout the tropics and subtropics, including Africa and the New World.

Oxytenanthera abyssinica or savanna bamboo, African in origin and found throughout much of the continent, is the bamboo used to make alcohol, especially in Tanzania, where bamboo wine is a celebrated local beverage. At the start of the rainy season (usually December), when the new bamboo shoots stand at about a meter high, their tips are cut off and, over the course of eight days, re-bruised, so that the sap oozes out. After collection, the sap quickly ferments, going from sweet to sour and strong in a few days. This sap and the resultant *pombe* (home brew) are called *ulanzi*. The Hehe people of Tanzania say that they discovered how to make *ulanzi* by watching the behavior of birds in the bamboo during the rainy season.

Savanna bamboo is the preferred bamboo species for use in acadja, a traditional acqua-culture system of Benin. The bamboo stakes, driven into the mud at the bottom of lagoons, become hosts for the green slime and mollusks fish love to feed on.

Bamboo is the favorite tree of Babalú-Ayé in Lukumí. In Yoruba-land it is used to make the fèrè or flute played by the trickster god Eshu. In Trinidad, tamboo bamboo, a trio of bamboo percussion instruments, became integral to the celebration of Carnival after the colonial government banned drums from the Canboulay processions. (See SUGARCANE)

Ulanzi

SOLO VOICE
I've just seen a bird
That couldn't touch the sky.
Why, why?
Tell me why!

VOICES
Too much bamboo sap.
Crashed out in the bush,
A necessary nap.

SOLO VOICE
Why, why?
Tell me why!

VOICES
Birds shouldn't drink and fly.

BANANA

Musa × sp., ndizi, matoke, figue
(banane), guineo

The banana, originally from Southeast Asia, arrived in Africa as part of the "monsoon exchange," the wind-assisted network of trade routes linking India and East Africa. Outside of the Global North, being yellow and sweet-tasting is far from the essence of the fruit. Even apart from the savory PLANTAIN, the "cooking banana" or *matoke* is a staple crop in Africa's Great Lakes region, coming in many different varieties and in shades from green to white. Some of these bananas are very starchy, saved for special occasions; more quotidian kinds are cooked into a variety of popular dishes alongside meat and peanuts; and yet other types are made into beer or hard liquor. Non-cooking, sweet varieties are grown in the region as well, and are consumed especially by children. Perhaps this is why

the *kinyamkela*, who is the ghost of a child, is so protective of his "yellow ones."

The Guinea Coast of Africa is where many Europeans first encountered the fruit and whence it came to the New World. The word "banana" itself is Wolof in origin, and yellow bananas are called *guineo* in parts of the Spanish-speaking Caribbean.

The story of the *kinyamkela* comes from the Zaramo people of Tanzania. Among the Haya, another Bantu group in Tanzania, the banana features in a ritual to support the growth of newborn children. Bananas loom large in diasporic traditions too: bananas with milk are the content of the diet of the bakru or baccoo of Suriname and Guyana, a darkly ambiguous spirit associated with wealth and empowered by ancient prejudice.

Kinyamkela

How were they to know
Those belonged to an ogre?
He of one leg
And solitary arm,
The one they call Kinyamkela.
How were they to know?
How were they to know
That those were his bananas?

He pelted them ceaselessly:
Mud missiles and stone,
Four days and nights,
Creating a cyclone:
Bombarded two frightened boys.

Took a bunch of Musa,
Also known as banana.
How were they to know?
How were they to know?
Those yellow ones belonged to a monster.

BAOBAB

Adansonia digitata, ose, ubuyu, yiri mango, kuka

The baobab tree is instantly recognizable by its thick, tapering trunk, which can sometimes be half as broad as the tree's considerable height. One legendary explanation for the baobab's odd shape is that the gods planted it upside down to curtail its arrogance. Thanks to that giant trunk, baobabs are among the largest living organisms, and individual trees can survive for thousands of years.

Baobabs originated in Africa, where, much like shea trees, they are cultivated in parklands for their shade, fruit, and leaves. The flesh of the fruit has an agreeable acidic taste, and its solid parts can be ground into flour; the leaves taste like spinach and are one of the most popular greens in West Africa. The seeds can also be used to thicken soups or made into candy. Almost every part of the tree has been put to practical use.

The baobab is the National Tree of Senegal and the home of the Konderongs, the little bearded ones who protect the forest. It also features in the Creation Story of the Hadza, the last of the hunter-gatherers of Tanzania. And for the Mikea, their counterparts in Madagascar, it is the residence of their ancestral spirits. The Zulu have used baobab powder as a test of truth.

The Baobab Monologue

I miss you,
Adansonia digitata.

I am Baobab,
So I sing of him,
Of the man who sat against me,
Contemplating tradition.
Root, branch, leaf, and fruit,
We sing of him,
Chanting "Birago Diop."

Not only me: everyone sings of him, animals and birds too, including Parrot. Whether in a squawk or in more dulcet tones, all the feathered ones want to add their voices in celebration. You see, they've heard how he treated chickens during his veterinary work, so they all want to chant words in homage to the one who took time to care.

So many have sat below these branches—lovers, picnic-eaters, practicing musicians, tired fisherman—but his is the only human name that I remember.

I felt like the chosen one as he rested his back against me,

his favored place of rest and meditation. Sometimes it'd be just him, Heron, Lizard and I: he loved being beside the water. Beyond the sense of soothing the slow-moving water gave him, he knew that across sub-Saharan Africa, rivers and lakes were the abode of the ancestors.

VOICES CHANTING
Whispering, listening,
Weaving of whispering,
Ancestors threading in and out.

BAOBAB
Yes, as much as he loved the river, he loved me; came here as often as the antelopes and the elephants. Whenever he went away, on his studies or for work, upon his return to Ouakam he always came here to greet me. I remember when he returned from France after the war. I'd never known him to be a religious man, but after kissing and embracing me, he knelt and prayed. And for the next hour, seated, he went from grinning to crying, crying to grinning, until a niece came looking for him, her favorite uncle. No, not a religious man, but I think of him as a spiritual one.

Yes, I have seen him weep and I have seen him laugh. Like the time he came back from one of his breaks from the school in Saint-Louis, weeping for the girl that he didn't get; Lizard croaked a dirge and this part of the river went quiet for a while. You see, he was our cherished one even then; he never threw stones at the birds, or battled the smaller animals with catapult. And speaking of his education, I'll always remember his jubilation at the news of his acceptance to study veterinary science at Toulouse University. He couldn't stop smiling. With the letter in his hand, he did a little victory dance, then sat against me, singing; and the birds within me, sensing his happiness, added their vocals in harmony; Heron bowed to him and he returned that respectful gesture.

That's all he wanted sometimes, just to lean against me and look upon the water. To him, that was very close to peace on Earth. He'd come here sometimes and let his thoughts flow out; I became a kind of sounding board for him. During wartime in France, in a letter to a friend, he addressed a thought to me. He spoke of the shrouding of light by a dark philosophy. His friend came and read it to me. Here is what it said, as I have retained it word for word.

> I wonder, Baobab, what will happen to the items of our traditions? What will the Nazis do with the Ngil mask and the Baule pendant? What will happen to the Ife Head and the Luba headrest? I have heard what they have done to the art by their own people—what will they do to ours? I wonder, have they taken out certain items from the museums in Dresden and Berlin? If so, will they do the same in the Museum of Man? Anyway, old friend, they can't take away Leuk the hare, Bouki the hyena and Golo the monkey; they are embedded where no one can touch them. Hope to see you soon, wise one; please give my respects to Heron and Lizard.

Yes, he would just sit here sometimes and let the words flow out. I heard the first draft of many of his poems, and "Souffles" is still my favorite.

Whispering, listening,
Weaving of whispering,
Ancestors threading in and out.

BAOBAB

I am privileged to have been present during some of the
sweetest conversation to pass human lips, like the time he
sat with Léopold Senghor, during their break from studies
in France. They spoke of everything: of Jean Price-Mars and
Nazi camps; of the master gewel and of their French tutors;
of Aimé Césaire and Jean-Paul Sartre; of the Mandinka and
Lebou; of independent Senegal. And while they spoke of
everything, hardly a sound was heard. The fluttering in the
branches ceased, Heron deferred his stalking, and Lizard
lay still on the trunk. Along this stretch of the river, we still
remember that conversation as Senghor Day.

And after his ambassadorship in Tunisia, he sat against
me and spoke of that North African country. He told me
of endless meetings and the need for patience, of couscous
and makroudh, and of the souks and the Zaytana Mosque;
but his conversation reached its crescendo when leaning
back against me, puffing on his pipe, he told me of Tunisian
folktales—of Akarek the tailor and of Zabra, lauded for her
beauty. He was older then, and finishing his working life
as a veterinary medic in his homeland.

We give what we can, don't we? My fruit I give as food
and medicine, my leaf as fodder for the animals and human
food in time of famine; I also store water in my trunk. He
gave also, of his skills, time, and that gargantuan heart—

saving the animals and enriching humanity.

He knew the value of stories, so he collected them wherever he went. From Burkina Faso, amongst the Mossi, stories of Mba-Soamba, the trickster hare. Mali produced one of the great epics of Africa, chronicling the deeds of Sunjata, hero of the Mandinka. After his return from Niger, I heard tales from the Hausa people: of Yan Dawa, the little people who protect the forest, and of Zankallala, always escorted by a group of birds—he's the small one who defeated Dodo the monster. From the Baule in Ivory Coast, the maneuverings of Anansi the spider. Mauretania gave him another great epic, the Dausi of the Soninke people. He brought them all back with him and we heard them all, Heron, Lizard, and I. I know as much about West African folklore as you do, dear reader.

He brought them all to me, so on many evenings, the river went to sleep with his voice: our soundtrack to lullaby time. But he has gone now, sitting amongst those he spoke of; they are happy he is there, because he held the torch and never let it go out.

VOICES CHANTING
Whispering, listening,
Weaving of whispering,
Ancestors threading in and out.

BAOBAB
He is gone from us now, but while he was here, he was the custodian of all that is worth saving. He spent a thousand moonlit hours chanting with the children. Now and again,

Heron, Lizard, and I will get together and reminisce; sometimes we'll weep a little and dry each others' tearfall. And
sometimes, when the river is at its quietest, we can hear the
gentle echo of his voice: and sometimes he chants of me...

VOICE CHANTING
I miss you,
Adansonia digitata.

BAOBAB
I am Baobab.
I'll always sing of him,
Of the man who sat against me,
Channeling ancestry.
Heron, Lizard and I,
We eulogize him,
Praising Birago Diop.

This piece is from The Birago Diop Trilogy, *published as a chapbook by Reamsworth
Publishing for secondary schools in Ibadan, Nigeria.*
*In the folklore of the Wolof of Senegal and Gambia, Leuk the hare, Bouki the hyena,
and Golo the monkey are three of the main characters.*

BASIL

efinrin, manjericão, albahaca, tignainti, efinrin, kloklotosu, *Ocimum* spp.

Adefetue, besobela, tulsi, lime basil: these are just a few members of the genus *Ocimum* besides the "sweet basil" of Italian cookery. Some are native to the Old World, others to the New, but most species are cosmopolitan today.

In Brazil, those who practice the African diasporic religions of Candomblé and Umbanda use them in in a purifying leaf bath, in which a priest kneads the leaves in cool water, then pours the water over a person who seeks to dispel negative energies or attract good fortune. Only the fresh leaves can be used, because it is the sap of a plant that contains its *axe* (ashe) or vital force. Basil and similar sweet-smelling herbs like basil are used in similar baths in the Winti religion of Suriname.

Followers of orisha religions like these, with their origins in Yoruba belief, might give basil as an offering to Obatala; his herbs are those that cleanse and purify. In Haitian Vodou practice, basil is often associated with the loas called Ezili or Erzulie, especialy Metres Erzulie Fréda, loa of love and luxury. It is used in Jamaica to ward off duppies (ghosts), and in the Dominican Republic, it is a customary ingredient in mamajuana, a beverage first made by the Indigenous Caribbean Taíno people. Here, basil and Mama Solace (introduced in ALFALFA) join forces to drive away bad energy.

The Companionship of Basil

She always seemed to be there—in spirit or flesh—just when you needed her. You see, she'd have these emanations, these outpourings of empathy, because soothing was her mission: the sacred objective. It would just flow from her, this need to comfort, to generate fortitude. This is why we call her Mama Solace.

Like the time when the woman came home from a day colored darkly—one of those days when the clock had gone into slow motion, the slowest shift ever known to Man; and the foreman had been in a scavenging mood, taking bits out of everyone. You can't blame his workforce for calling him the Vulture. Then after she'd left work, a shopping cart wheel had gone over her foot in the supermarket and she couldn't get a seat on the bus home.

As she stepped through the front door, she dropped the shopping bags like she'd been shouldering all the troubles of the known world.

Then Mama Solace came to her, chanting in her head:

> Your day has been torment,
> Sapping your will.
> Put your feet in the water,
> Your time of reward,

Pamper your feet with basil.

And as she came into the living room, a smile blazed across her face for the first time that day, transforming it completely after the pickings of the Vulture: there was her beloved husband, mashing basil leaves in a large bowl of water while making a request...

"As I keep my arms around her, please watch over her, Mama Solace. May tiredness slump away and may the evening bring respite. May food revitalize her and sleep strengthen her. My love for her is always."

That's how it is with Mama Solace; all her positivity, all the support she gives, comes from flora. Which is why some people call her Mama Ewe (eh-weh): ewe is the Yoruba word for plants.

A little while later, the woman, still smiling, after giving thanks to the Creator, gave thanks for her husband, for Mama Solace, and for a newfound companion called Basil.

BLUE LOTUS

sacred blue lily of the Nile, seshen, *Nymphaea caerulea*

The flower of this lotus (or water lily, strictly speaking) comes in hues ranging from white to pinkish mauve to the striking sky blue of its name. Its pointed petals are arranged in a delicate star shape, and, as you will soon learn, it smells heavenly. It grows along the Nile and throughout East and Southern Africa; though less abundant today than in antiquity, it has been found thriving even in nutrient-deficient lakes, often alongside WATER CABBAGE.

Two water lily species were sacred to the ancient Egyptians and appear everywhere in their art. One, the Egyptian white lotus, blooms at night, while the slightly smaller blue lotus opens its buds in the morning and closes them at dusk. For this reason, the blue lotus was associated with the Sun and the Sun God as well as with rebirth. King Tutankhamun's body, when found in its tomb in 1922, was still garlanded with the 3000-year-old petals of blue lotus, and near him was a carving depicting the boy-king as the god Nefertem, being reborn out of the blue lotus flower.

Black Lotus

SONIA: So tell me, why the recent interest in aromatherapy?

RUBY: The Blue Lotus.

SONIA: The water lily?

RUBY: Yes.

SONIA: Why?

RUBY: Well, for a few reasons. Now, you know how when we're testing or wearing perfume, we might say it's "divine." Well, concerning the lotus, it's true, because in ancient Egypt it was a sacred flower. Can't wait to smell it! I've been digging into the old Egyptian stories: wicked! Apparently, one time when the god Ra was in serious pain (don't know whether it was mental or physical), Nefertem brought him a bouquet of blue lotus, which is said to have brought him some soothing.

SONIA: Just the thing, then, when Marlon is doing my head in!

RUBY: You're always running that man, when we all know he's gentle and patient.

SONIA: I know, but you know how I am.

RUBY: Yes, I do! Now back to the water lily.

SONIA: Ok. So who's this Nefe, Nefeta—

RUBY: Nefertem. He's sunrise. He is the deity representing life, as the first human came forth from a blue lotus flower—his iconic headwear—on that primordial morning.

SONIA: Yes! I'm with you now. So that yellow gold bit in the middle of the flower represents the sun.

RUBY: Exactly! Yellow sun in the petal blue sky, opening in the morning, closing again at night.

SONIA: Like us.

RUBY: Yes, like us.

SONIA: Beautiful.

RUBY: Like us.

SONIA: Smell better than us!

RUBY: That's true also. Always good to walk by that pool, lower down on the river, and get a waft of the lilies before moving on: a little treat for the nasal zone.

SONIA: I was thinking of them as counteraction, antidote, after Marlon's bombarded the toilet bowl! Or would that be stretching lotus a little too far? Might send our little blue friend into retirement, never to bloom again. The struggle with Marlon's odor might kill off the lotus's!

RUBY: Poor Marlon!

SONIA: Poor Marlon! You mean poor me! He never rises to my teasing and taunting. He's always quiet and cool like that damn lotus! But joking aside, I do agree with you. It's good to get a waft of lily aroma when passing that pool. And that Ra must have been glad just at the sight of the bouquet. Yes, my friend, joking aside, you know Marlon is my water lily. His positivity and calmness help me through the day from the minute it begins.

RUBY: We all know he's your sunshine.

SONIA: He is my Black Lotus.

BOUGAINVILLEA

Bougainvillea spp., bougainville, sempre-lustrosa, três-marias, santa rita, trinitaria

All year long, if conditions are right, the bougainvillea vine (really a LIANA, a woody, climbing shrub) is graced with impossibly vibrant blooms—most often magenta, but also orange, purple, white, and even rose-colored ones that turn white as they age. The bright "petals" are actually bracts, specialized leaves, like on poinsettias. If you look closely, you can see the true flower they enclose, a minute tube topped by five whitish petals. Its nectar is beloved by hummingbirds, who are able to reach their beaks past the bracts.

A French plantswoman named Jeanne Baret, who in 1766 circumnavigated the globe dressed as a man, was likely the first European to encounter bougainvillea. She collected it in its native Brazil, near Rio de Janeiro. A century and a half later, Kate Sessions, the horticulturist best known as the "mother" of San Diego's Balboa Park, championed bougainvillea to Californians. The flower is now celebrated in festivals from India to Australia and throughout the Caribbean.

Bougainvillea is the flower associated with Damballah, one of the great spirits, called *loa* or *lwa*, of Vodou belief. He is the husband (or brother, depending on the tradition) of the *loa* Ayida-Wedo, who represents the rainbow.

Bougainvillea Prayer

Ahhh, Damballah. Who better to associate with bougainvillea iridescence? You, foundation and protector of our
residence, let me drape you in magenta.

Giving thanks for the flame tree,
Let me dress you in orange.
Giving thanks for oriole,
Let me swathe you in yellow.
Giving thanks for hibiscus,
Let me wrap you in red.
Giving thanks for coconut,
Let me sheathe you in white.
Giving thanks for glossy ibis,
Let me fold you in purple.

Instigator of all the blessings, first facilitator of
color: only you, Damballah, wearer of the rainbow we
call bougainvillea.

For Petra Bakewell-Stone

BREADFRUIT

Artocarpus altilis, pana, panapen, masapan, afon

Breadfruit is the compound fruit of a tall, large-leafed tree in the mulberry family, sibling of the very similar jackfruit. A breadfruit consists of a number of different fleshy growths which have merged together, each of which may or may not contain a seed, depending on the cultivar. Seedless varieties have to be spread by human beings who carry suckers and cuttings from place to place. The presence of seedless breadfruits from Madagascar to Polynesia shows how they spread with human migration out of Southeast Asia thousands of years ago.

Disregarding the starchy tubers that enslaved Africans were already growing in their provision grounds, colonial bioprospectors looked to breadfruit as a source of cheap and plentiful carbohydrate with which to fuel slave labor. It was for this purpose that breadfruit first traveled from Polynesia to the Americas—on the ship of William Bligh, captain of HMAV *Bounty*. The precious breadfruit cuttings taken on board the *Bounty* in Tahiti occupied the captain's quarters; when Bligh's men mutinied and took over the ship, they threw the cuttings into the sea. But Bligh, having survived the mutiny, returned to Tahiti on a second voyage and managed to bring the fruit to Jamaica.

Boiled, fried, roasted, or ground into a flour, breadfruit is now part of cuisines all over Africa, the Caribbean, and Latin America. Breadfruit can be offered to the orisha Obatala, among others.

Breadfruit and Marbles

They call me *Artocarpus*. In fact, my full name is *Artocarpus altilis*. Apparently, this name was given to me by a Swedish man, to help with international recognition of me. I appreciate that *Artocarpus altilis* is quite a mouthful, so please call me Breadfruit.

Tell me, have you ever been to St. Vincent and the Grenadines? Thirty-two islands where the Spirit of Beauty passed through, stayed awhile, then left her imprint. I sit high up in the tree, entranced by what she has left us. They say my ancestral home in the Pacific was also visited by the Spirit of Beauty, but I can only take the word of the ones who've been there.

But I can speak of here, looking over Wallilabou River. And in August here they celebrate my contribution to all that the eye can see.

People and I have a long, deep connection. I have been their staple since the 18th century, and because they celebrate release from chains in August, I am freedom fruit. I feel honored to be celebrated in the same month that people commemorate their emancipation.

It is the month of the little champion also. Which child will enter the annals of neighborhood folklore as the legendary victor of marbles? They will graduate to cart

48

racing and cricket, but for now, they yearn to wear the crown in the court of diminutive kings.

Focused visage,
Immersed in glass ball strategy:
His turn to roll now,
Another boy of scuffed knee.
Scowl of frustration?
Dance of victory?
I hope he sings,
"La da da da da da dee."
A plate will be waiting,
Full of breadfruit cookies
Singing la da da da da da dee.

CALABASH

igbá, wamdé, *Lagenaria siceraria*, bottle gourd

There is a Yoruba saying that two halves of a calabash make a universe. This saying contains a complex cosmology, but it could as well refer to calabash's omni-presence in diaspora culture. In "Calabash Man," the calabash takes the form of the bendré, a drum of deep importance to the Mossi people of Burkina Faso. A calabash with a long neck might be made into the side-blown trumpet called the upe, played at the festival of Ogun, or it might become a shere, a rattle used by devotees of the orisha of thunder-storms, Shango. In Brazil, the calabash serves as the resonator of the berimbau, an instrument with African roots, which today accompanies performances of the martial arts dance *capoeira* as well as Candomblé rites. Calabashes may be made into vessels, ordinary or (as in "African Lettuce") cere-monial; into fishermen's buoys; and into tools for divination, among countless other roles.

Calabashes, originally African, drifted across the sea thousands of years ago, joining ARROWROOT to become one of the oldest culti-vated plants in South America. Such long use has led to confusing nomenclature: in West Africa, the calabash plant is a true gourd, a vine like cucumber, also known as "bottle gourd." In the Caribbean and parts of South America, cala-bashes can come from a different plant, *Crescentia cujete,* a small evergreen tree. These inedible calabashes grow directly on the tree-trunk, and the flowers are pollinated by bats, like the baobab's. Finally, "calabash" may be a translation of the Spanish *calabaza,* a squash or pumpkin.

In the World-Calabash of Yoruba religion, the top half, the sky or heaven, is Obatala; the bottom half, earth, is Oduduwa; and the force that holds the two halves together is *ashe.*

Calabash Man

I see you, Birago, in the evening time, after your day of dealing with a sheep disease—your back against a silk cotton tree, surrounded by the grateful residents, while the storyteller plays the drum of his name and craft, bendré: calabash. The chief must value you highly—as do the people—to have the bendré played.

Calabash,
Calabash,
Burkina Faso.
Calabash,
Calabash,
In Tankudugo:
Story of Mba-Kaongo.

I see you, Birago, your face illuminated by the fire, puffing on your pipe, smiling, as fireflies flit, the breeze massages one and all, and the little ones begin to get sleepy.

Calabash,
Calabash,
Burkina Faso.
Calabash,
Calabash,

In Tankudugo:
Story of Mba-Wobgo.

Mba-Kaongo, the guinea fowl, features in a Mossi story about water and karma; Mba-Wobgo, the elephant, in one concerning romantic rivalry.

CASSAVA

manioc, yuca, *Manihot esculenta*, kpaki

Cassava or manioc, found in foods as American as apple pie, as Asian as bubble tea, and as African as fufu, began its journey around the world in the Caribbean. The Taíno inhabitants of that region were among the Meso- and South-American peoples to invent ways of turning the cyanide-containing tubers of the plant into foods, like cassava flour and the starch we know by its Tupí-Guaraní name, tapioca.

The Taíno interplant the cassava shrub with other crops, like arrowroot and peanut, in dense, diverse mounded garden plots called *conucos* which have been cleared by slash-and-char techniques. After harvest, the roots are grated, placed in a long tubular basket to squeeze out the juice from the pulp, and then kneaded on a *metate* (flat millstone.) The resultant flour can be baked into the crispy *casabe* flatbread integral to Taíno cuisine, now widespread in the greater Caribbean. Within seventy years of Columbus's first encounter with the Taíno on the island he called Hispaniola, cassava had reached Africa, where it would become a staple crop, for many as important as rice and corn. It's now an ingredient in tasty street foods and in desserts like the Nigerian pudding mingau.

The Taíno creator god Yúcahu is the "giver of cassava" and master of the sea. The Tupí of the Amazon tell of how a child called Maní became the source and eponym of manioc. In African diasporic religions, cassava can be offered to Papa Legba and to Ogun; in Candomblé, manioc flour may be part of an offering to the trickster orisha Exu (Eshu.) And in Ghana, cassava leaf is used as a talisman, especially for matters of love.

53

The Manioc Mantra

I sometimes ask myself, why me? Why not Okra, Pumpkin or Eggplant? Why my leaves? I mean, I'm supposed to be toxic to them, so why me? I feel like the chosen one, but it comes with pressure. Who needs pressure? Wish I could be like Watermelon, Yam, or one of the others; grown, consumed, enjoyed; that's it, no pressure. But no, some person back in time—healer, mystic, forest guardian, I don't know—decided I was the one to facilitate rekindled love. Let me tell you how it goes.

A woman who's with an Elsewhere Man goes early in the morning to where I'm located, picks my leaves, soaks them in salted water, and after three days places them under the pillow of the man. So you can see the pressure I'm under as she quietly chants:

> Cassava leaves,
> Under his pillow,
> Time to rekindle the glow.

She wants to go smiling again through Kumasi Market, stopping here and there, buying this and that, arm in arm through the colorful scene. To sit snuggled, joking as they used to, laughing easily. Like the time he shared a tale about

Sasabonsam, he of iron teeth and iron feet—when, removing themselves from the sofa, they roleplayed an encounter between a forest walker and the aforementioned ogre; she played the forest walker, fearless warrior, vanquishing old Metalmouth.

And after the rekindling to go to Lake Bosomtwi, giving thanks to Nyame. Then to return, to sit at their favourite chop bar, enjoying jubilation jollof. Until then, she places hope in me, quietly chanting:

> Cassava leaves,
> Under his pillow,
> Time to rekindle the glow.

Sasabonsam is a monster of Ashanti folklore, resident of trees who dangles his branching, vine-like legs, ready to ensnare unwary travelers. Nyame is the Ashanti name for the Creator (remember, there were monotheistic beliefs throughout sub-Saharan Africa before the coming of Islam and Christianity.)

CHAMOMILE

German chamomile, *Matricaria recutita*, margaça-das-boticas, manzanilla alemana

Most of us have sipped or at least smelled the gently honey-scented tea of the chamomile plant. The herb itself has soft, feathery leaves and flowerheads that look like tiny daisies, with white petals and yellow centers; this is the part used to make the tea. The essential oil of chamomile is a surprising deep blue: it contains a derivative of the compound azulene, a powerful anti-inflammatory. The ancient Egyptians used the plant medicinally and ritually, offering it to the sun god Ra and anointing the body of the pharaoh Ramses II with chamomile oil after his death.

The genus *Matricaria* contains several plants with similar fragrance and properties. *Matricaria pubescens* or *ouazouaza* is a common medicine in the northern Sahara, while *Matricaria discoidea*, "pineapple weed," is a diminutive ruderal species found in lawns and ditches throughout North America and Europe.

In diasporic practices and beyond, chamomile is used as a calming herb; it generates mental wellbeing and soothes insomnia and nightmares. Chamomile is offered to the orisha Oshun, who guards all rivers—from her namesake in Nigeria (see AFRICAN LETTUCE) to Oxford's Thames.

Tale of Chamomile

He said the two things she loved were chamomile and rivers. Jah Folk was talking about a fellow folklorist, an English woman he'd met at a conference in London many years before. They'd kept in contact, developing friendship and collaborating professionally. Now she was having a nervous breakdown.

We sat in the square—grandchild, grandparent, and all ages in between—as the breeze came through, talking of mental health: episodes, medicine, discrimination, therapies, dignity, doctors, loneliness and hospitals. We spoke of those unfulfilled, of the searchers who are suffering.

I think it was cathartic for some gathered there. Talking of support networks—creative writing workshops, food sharing, dominoes club, gardening—rather than stigmatization. Discussing ways to help strengthen the ones experiencing fragility. We heard beautiful terms like bolstering and boosting. It was good to sit there, gently addressing a subject often thought taboo. I remember that everyone left quietly that night, or in muted conversation, reflecting on the evening's conversation. But before we dispersed, Jah Folk told us of a receiver of chamomile, Oshun, an orisha of rivers and love. Then he recited Offering Chamomile.

Going to where the heron stands
And Kingfisher passes by;
Across the meadow,
Over the stile,
And in my bag,
A gift of chamomile.

As Papa Bwa of the forest,
She is a guardian of rivers;
So I'll sit by the Thames
In a little while,
Chanting for Oshun,
Offering Chamomile.

Jah Folk, *a folklorist and storyteller based in Kingston, made his first appearance as the mouthpiece of Rootical Folklore in my collection* The Papine Tales, *published online in 2022 by Jamaica's Wisemind Publications. Of an evening, he hosts the Moonlit Classroom in Papine Square. "Moonlit Classroom" is my term for the traditional intergenerational gatherings where children first learn the lessons of life around the evening fire. Each evening focuses on a different item of flora. In this one, it's Chamomile; in the tale following, it's Chaney Root.*

CHANEY ROOT

Smilax balbisiana, China root, briar withe, cocolmeca, atacorral

In the Jamaican tradition of Roots Tonic, knowledgeable people, often Rastafari elders, collect bark, roots, and vines from the forest, which they make into a drink that imparts strength and vitality. You can buy the tangy brown-colored drink, often sold in reused Campari and Wray bottles, from roadsides, restaurants, and shops; some say it tastes rather like sorrel. The ingredients of Roots Tonic vary from one herbalist to another, but no matter what else may be added to the mix, two foundational ingredients are SARSAPA-RILLA and chaney root.

These two closely related plants, members of the widely distributed greenbrier family, are prickly vines with glossy, heart-shaped leaves. The name "chaney

root" is a variant of "China root," the English name for a *Smilax* species native to Asia that was imported to Europe in great quantities as a syphilis treatment starting in the sixteenth century. Jamaica's chaney root, however, is endemic to the island. It grows all over, but is most common in "Cockpit Country," the rugged and hilly rainforests of Western Jamaica. This area was a strong-hold of the self-liberated Maroons, who formed thriving communities in this wild country, sustaining and healing themselves by relying on African traditions and likely on botanical knowledge shared by the Indigenous Taíno. In this way, Roots Tonic has to do with self-determination, resistance, and the ancestral sense of "roots."

Chaney Root Chant

It was an evening of gratitude, an evocation. We sat in Papine Square, giving thanks for sarsaparilla and chaney. We had all said our private eulogies to the two, but this was a public utterance, a collective salute. At some point, we'd all had the support of the twosome, felt that their partnership had come to our individual aid. As well as for the plants, we gave thanks for the local Rastamen, such as Shanty Man and Dr. Spice, who used both in the making of Roots Tonic. We joined in the chanting and discussion points enthusiastically, enjoying the impromptu celebration of two from the genus Smilax.

And he presented them to us as a monologue, calling himself Brother Chaney, presenting Sarsaparilla, his sister. I always asked Jah Folk to write out the poems and chants for me, and later on I requested them via email.

> *Smilax,*
> *Smilax,*
> No need to pay a tax;
> So come and dig for me,
> *Smilax balbisiana.*
> I am Brother Chaney.

CHERRY

capulín, capolcuahuitl, *Prunus serotina*

The cherry tree native to Mexico's high plateaus, the capulín, is the same species as the wild cherry or black cherry common in the deciduous forests of North America and Europe, but taxonomists were slow to realize this. Over centuries of selection and cultivation, the region's inhabitants, including the Nahua and Otomí people, had altered the plant almost beyond recognition. They made the fruits larger and sweeter, and the pits, which like those of most *Prunus* species contain cyanogens when raw, more palatable: roasted and salted, even the pits can be transformed into a delicacy. Striking purple *tamales de capulín* are still a special treat in August and September, when the fruits are at their peak.

The cherry plays a part in many of the landscapes of traditional Mexican agriculture: in family gardens; in floating *chinampas*; in an agroecosystem called *metepantl*, a polyculture featuring agave plants; and in multistory rainfed plots where trees, interplanted with corn, increase organic matter in the soil, capture moisture and nutrients, and prevent erosion. The tree also grows wild, and it is common in the mountains ringing the so-called "cuenca cimmarón" or "maroon watershed" near Veracruz. In these mountains, Africans who had freed themselves from slavery on the Veracruz plantations formed communities called *palenques*, starting in the 16th century with those led by Gaspar Yanga. The Yanguicos made farms in the mountains, and from time to time, they surely also gathered wild cherries.

Cherries can be a gift to Oba, orisha of the river that carries her name.

Cherry Temptation

Tomato went to get water,
Cherry tree
For the elderly couple,
Cherry tree,
La la la,
Dee dee dee,
Everything tempted by the cherry tree.

Onion went to get water,
Cherry tree,
Old people still waiting,
Cherry tree,
La la la,
Dee dee dee,
Everything tempted by the cherry tree.

Chili went to get water,
Cherry tree,
The seniors wilting,
Cherry tree,
La la la,
Dee dee dee,

Everything tempted by the cherry tree.

The old ones go themselves,
Cherry tree,
Gorging there on the fruit,
Cherry tree,
La la la,
Dee dee dee,
Everything tempted by the cherry tree.

From a tale from Mexico, "The Wild Cherry Tree," this is a song for lovers of cherries—
and a reminder that sometimes we have to help ourselves rather than depend on others.

CHILI PEPPER

chilli, ají, pimenta-malagueta, *Capsicum* spp., ata [sombo, rodo, ijosi], pripíri

Chili peppers come in many different shapes, sizes, and colors, but all of them are the fruit of a species in the genus *Capsicum*, which has been distributed through the Americas for more than fifty million years. The plants' domestication began in South and Central America some seven thousand years ago. They were a big part of Mesoamerican cuisine; for the Mexica, who named it *chilli*, the plant acted as a charm and a ritual tool for worshiping Tlaloc, the rain god.

Europeans first met *Capsicum* in the Antilles, where the Taíno people cultivated spicy varieties of what they called *axi*—a plant they had brought, like ARROWROOT, from the Orinoco Delta via canoe. The peppers were an ingredient in a stew called casiripe, made of CASSAVA juice along with meat,

fish, shellfish, and vegetables. By the nineteenth century, the same dish had come to the US, prepared and sold on the streets of Philadelphia by Black women known as "pepperpot women," some of the nation's first street vendors. A very different cinnamon-spiked version of the dish is the traditional Christmas morning stew in the Guyanas to this day.

The Portuguese spread hot peppers globally, including to India, where some Europeans came to believe the plant had originated, and to their Southern African territories, where they grew piri-piri, a cultivar of the malagueta Afro-Brazilians used in lieu of ALLIGATOR PEPPER.

Hot peppers can be offered to Shango, the orisha of lightning, and left at the temple of Babalú-Ayé, orisha of disease and healing.

Tale of Chili Pepper

Jah Folk liked taking us, the evening listeners in Papine Square, to Puerto Rico—like that night he told us about Pura Belpré and shared one of the stories this legendary storyteller used to tell the children who'd gather around her in the library on 115th Street in Harlem: a tale of a plant and a witch.

This demonic entity was one of those who led a double life, like the one called soucouyants in other Caribbean islands. During the day, she'd potter around, dealing with domesticity; then, when the night stepped in, she'd shed her skin and go off again, on another campaign of mayhem.

If there was such a thing as a degree in Human Transformation Studies, she would have come through with honors. Probably have written an award-winning thesis, entitled "Nocturnal Metamorphosis." In the fraternity of shapeshifters, I can imagine she was lauded as a don.

But what of the human element? What of smell? You see, the nostrils of her new husband had been detecting sulfur in the morningtime bedroom. Also, he'd noticed that his beloved was tired when she woke, further arousing his suspicions. Can't blame him, with his wife smelling like a chemistry lab and looking like she'd just done hard labor on a night shift! So one night he feigns sleep and peeks out from under the covers when she arises. Then, he watches open-mouthed, goggle-eyed, petrified, screaming silently, as she sheds her skin. He watches as she flies away like a combusting fireball into the darkness, and realizes the source of the sulfur.

Coming out of his shock, he gathers all the chili peppers in the house together and rubs them into the discarded item. On her return, re-dressing herself in her skin, she experiences another burning; she scratches, curses, jumps around, writhes on the floor, and then she is still. Her witching days are done; her husband throws her lifeless body in a ditch.

I remember to this day the exuberance with which we children voiced the "Chili Pepper Chant," chanting with the children of Puerto Rico:

> Gave thanks for Bolivia,
> For chili pepper,
> Defeating sorceress.
> Pepper, pepper,
> We love you, pepper:
> Ceasing the midnight distress.

> Gave thanks for Bolivia,
> For chili pepper,
> We defeated the witch.
> Pepper, pepper,
> We love you, pepper:
> Slung her body in the ditch.

CLOVES

cravo-da-índia, kanafuru, *Syzygium aromaticum,* syn. *Eugenia caryophyllata*

Cloves grow on evergreen trees that bear clusters of waxy red flowers. The buds of these flowers, picked when they are still a pink-green color, are dried to become the familiar spice. The tree is native to the Maluku Islands in Indonesia, but Austronesian sailors traded cloves over vast distances, from Taiwan to Madagascar, from as early as the second millennium BCE.

It is said that the clove tree must be able to see the ocean, and it has been grown successfully only on islands or near the coast. One such coastal region where cloves are cultivated today, far from their original home, is Bahia, the Brazilian state home to the most Brazilians of African descent and the birthplace of the African diasporic religion Candomblé. Candomblé and its sister religion, Umbanda, both use sacred herbs in various types of baths (see also ROSEMARY.) This piece is an invitation to use cloves as an Umbanda practitioner might, for purification and to raise one's energy levels. In Umbanda, cloves might be offered to the orixás (orishas) Iansã (Oya) and to Oxum (Oshun), amongst others.

Cloves Energizer

You're looking drained.
The day was too long—
Come put your feet in the water.
Time to energize;
Let the spirits rise;
Come put your feet in the water
Embellished by ashe from cloves.

Ashe *(pronounced ah-shay) is the essence, the force, that all living things possess.*

COCONUT

Cocos nucifera, agbon, noix de coco, nux indica

The coconut is a tropical palm tree–a member of the family *Arecaceae*, like the DATE PALM and the oil PALM. The fruit we buy in stores is actually the pit, like an almond, of a much larger fruit; the outer part of this fruit is composed of a tough fiber known as coir, from which such products as rope, rugs, and soil amendments are made.

Thousands of years ago, people living in the islands of Southeast Asia and the Indian Ocean separately began to cultivate the coconut tree. Ancient Austronesian mariners transported coconuts, along with others like PLANTAIN and TARO, far across the Pacific, as well as eastward to Madagascar and coastal East Africa. The fruits also dispersed themselves along the ocean currents, their tough shells protecting them from saltwater.

All Lukumí rituals begin with an offering of coconut, and they are used as kola nuts are in Yorubaland, in a form of divination called obí. The coconut shell is cut or broken into four pieces and tossed to perform a reading. Coconut may also be used in a "head prayer," a ceremony that cools and cleanses the ori. Coconut belongs to the great orisha Obatala, who owns the obí oracle and is linked to the color white.

Chant of the Coconut

You made a poor choice,
Little Ground Dove:
You should have chosen me.
Genus Cocos,
Instead of cedar:
Should have chosen the coconut tree.

You bet Mountain Dove
Who could live longer;
You began to feel hungry.
Chose a tree out of fruit,
Mountain Dove more astute:
Should have chosen the coconut tree.

You lost the wager,
Death took you away,
Without a route to Plan B:
Mislaid common sense,
Thinking became dense:
Should have chosen the coconut tree.

For Denise Amory-Reid.
The theme of two birds in a fasting contest is a popular one throughout African and Caribbean orality, found in countries such as Nigeria, Gabon, and the Congo, as well as in Jamaica, Haiti and Puerto Rico.

CUCUMBER

Cucumis sativus, *Cucumis anguria*, maxixe, concombre, pepino cimarrón, ihalabujana

The slicing cucumber got its start in Asia—Nepal, India, or Burma—and was originally just as bitter as its cousin BALSAM APPLE before people began to domesticate it, 3000 years ago. It likely arrived in North Africa in medieval times and from there, during the Ummayad Caliphate, reached southern Europe. The cuke landed in Haiti with Columbus; by the time Jacques Cartier voyaged to Montreal forty years later, he found the local people growing them there.

A rather different cucumber came to the Caribbean from southeast Africa via Brazil, likely brought by enslaved people: the West Indian burr gherkin or "maroon cucumber" (*C. anguria*), which became so abundant in the Antilles that Europeans thought it had originated there. The spiny, egglike fruits make excellent pickles, though they can also be cooked in the style of squash; called *maxixe* in Brazil (from the Bantu language Kimbundu), they feature in the Bahian stew *maxixada*. In dry regions of East Africa, this gherkin, which can grow wild on the Kalahari sand, is a popular and valuable species, along with the similar but orange "horned" cucumber *C. metuliferus*. The leaves and seeds are eaten as well.

In Lukumí, the burr gherkin is a plant of the strong and fiery Oya.

Tale of Chi Wara

Week of the Masquerade—that's it! I remember now, that's what they called it. Not Masking Week, or Days of the Mask. Anyway, that week Jah Folk, our local hero, stepped into Papine High, talking of the Bamana, chanting Chi Wara, during our week celebrating African masking traditions.

So there he was, the smile on his face competing for radiance with the red-gold-green halo adorning his head and his silver glistening beard. His enthusiasm igniting all—staff as well as students—he told us of the Bamana, founders of the great states of Segu and Kaarta. Of bogolanfani, one of the famed cloths of West Africa, decorated with fermented mud. Of their Creation Story, involving a shea tree.

The deity Chi Wara—depicted as a fusion of antelope, pangolin, and aardvark—was their agricultural teacher: the one who facilitated their introduction to farming. He taught the rudiments to the Bamana ancestors so all could have sorghum and millet. Bread and porridge for everyone. Beer for libation and the relaxation of adults.

Talking further about grain, he led us into a discussion of dumplings! Preferences for corn or oat? Fried or boiled? If fried, with salt fish and ackee, or scrambled egg and beans? If boiled, more of yam or green banana? If oat, with coconut flavoring or not? And everyone had something to say, sparkling with recipes and grandmothers' magic. Personally, I prefer oat dumplings and always welcome a coconut embellishment.

Laughter had to be curtailed; time began to withdraw its support. But before finishing with the Bamana chant—everyone standing—he told us that Mali, home of the Bamana, was the largest producer of cucumber in West Africa.

Chi Wara,
Please come amongst us,
Teach us of agriculture.

Chi Wara,
Tell us of seasons,
When to grow cucumber.

Chi Wara,
Herald of blessings,
Pathway ancestor.

The Bamana are one of the Mande peoples found throughout West Africa. Bassekou Kouyate, thought of as the greatest living exponent of ngoni, one of the traditional instruments of the jali or griot, is Bamana.

CYPRESS

ahuehuetl (ahuehuete), sabino, Montezuma cypress, *Taxodium mucronatum*

With its majestic size and brooding, ancient presence, it's no wonder the Montezuma cypress is named for an emperor. In Nahuatl oratory, the role of the Aztec ruler was often compared to the combined shade cast by this tree and the KAPOK. The first humans of Aztec mythology, Tata and Nene, took shelter from the Great Flood inside one of these trees. It is now the national tree of Mexico, where it is called the ahuehuete, and many members of the species still draw crowds and inspire reverence throughout the country. One ahuehuete, in the town of of Dolores Hidalgo, is the offspring of a tree under which Cortés is said to have wept after Aztecs defeated his forces on the so-called "Noche Triste." Another, the 1,500-year-old Árbol del Tule near Oaxaca, holds the title of "world's stoutest tree"; according to tradition, it was planted by the wind god Ehecatl.

Ahuehuetl means "old man of the water" in Nahuatl, and water is indeed dear to these trees. In the floating gardens of the Nahua, called chinampas, these trees were the keystone: they were planted in the mud and their roots held the entire island together. Today, it's common to see age-old ahuehuetes on dry ground; they mark the former sites of rivers and lagoons. But chinampas still grow; ahuehuetes still line many waterways; and they say that in the still of night, you can sometimes hear the trees in conversation, sharing the stories of time.

The Cypress Philosophers

He looks, then returns his eyes to the pathway. He sees their relishing of squash and tomato, the back and forth of laughter. Then one of the children removes herself from the little firelit gathering to give bits of watermelon to her favorite dog. Lucky dog! He glimpses planet Hearth, then returns to his own.

He goes down by the river to where the cypress trees have held their corner for more than two thousand years. The young man knows the tale of aeons: that sometimes, in the stillness of the night, these "old men of the water" converse with each other, sharing the ancient stories.

As the night begins its daily gnawing, he sits amongst the elders, his back against one, listening, as the wise ones of Atoyac River commence their evening seminar.

DATES

k'enochi, tamaro, *Phoenix dactylifera*

Dates grow on a palm tree that rises up to 100 feet in height. Flower spikes emerge from near the top of the tree, and these eventually grow clusters of the red and yellow fruit from which those brownish dried dates best known in the US and Europe are produced. While the fruits are growing, date farmers trim the clusters to ensure that the remaining dates grow fleshy. Then they bag the clusters in mesh to make sure that birds don't fly off with their harvest.

Dates are among the oldest domesticated plants, having first been farmed in the Indus Valley and Arabia as early as the sixth millennium BCE. They grow well in loose, sandy soils and in high-sun, low-rain climates. By the Middle Ages, date palms had spread throughout the Middle East and North Africa, including the parts of Sudan where the Nuer people live.

In places where they grow, dates are eaten fresh as well as dried. A syrup and a wine can be made by crushing the fruits, and tapping the trees themselves yields a sweet sap. The Spanish likely tried to introduce date palms to the Caribbean, but they don't produce well in such a rainy climate. Dates can be given to Aganju, orisha of the natural forces of the earth.

Tale of Dates

And there was the night we spoke of Paradise. Jah Folk put out the question, asking of content. If you could take a supply of one item to your idea of paradise, what would you take? Answers came in, such as music, books, make-up, clothing, and so on. He told us that if Kulang Toat was asked the same question, his answer would probably be dates. But before dates, he introduced Kulang.

You see, when we think of central characters in folk tales, we tend to think of animals first, such as Mbe, tortoise of Igbo folktales; Sungura, hare of Swahili stories; and Anansi, spider of the Ashanti. But there are human figures also, such as Tere from the Banda of the Central African Republic, Yogbo from the Fon of Benin, and Kulang from the Nuer of South Sudan. They meander through the moonlight stories. Kulang Toat was a historical personage who became a leading presence in Nuer oral traditions.

So one morning, a trader comes from Dongola to where Kulang resides in Fangak, carrying a large sack on his head. After offloading, he offers Kulang a sample of his wares. Kulang is hooked! From then on, all he thinks of is Dongola.

And here our local hero invited us to chant with him. So we chanted the name of the town in traditional call

and response:

> Vision in his head,
> Dongola.
> Twenty-four seven,
> Dongola.
> Whether by foot,
> Dongola.
> Or via camel,
> Dongola.
> He's got to go to
> Dongola.

Having sold a cow, then joined a group of traders, Kulang makes the two-month journey to his kiss-the-ground destination. Once he steps into his Promised Land, he doesn't want to leave: dates everywhere! Jolted out of his two-day reverie by the thought of his wife and children, he eats a few more dates, then reluctantly leaves Salivation Street, carrying as many as he and the camel can manage, eager to begin growing and trading them back in his homeland.

Jah Folk concluded, saying that in the oral traditions, as Anansi is credited with accidentally introducing sorrel drink, Kulang is seen as the pioneering figure of date cultivation in South Sudan.

The Nuer are one of the Nilotic peoples—which includes the more well-known Maasai. They live a life in which cattle are paramount.
See HIBISCUS *for the story of Anansi and sorrel.*

EGGPLANT

(e)ntula, jinjilo, njilu, n[j]akati, garden egg,
Solanum aethiopicum "Gilo", white brinjal

Solanum is a large genus of tropical plants that includes tomatoes, potatoes, nightshades, and eggplants. The plant bearing the purple fruits found on Western grocery store shelves, *Solanum melongena*, is not the only species called "eggplant." Another is *Solanum macrocarpon*, or Gboma eggplant, which bears small green or orange fruits, as well as leaves that in Nigeria and Benin are often cooked with ACKEE.

There's also *Solanum aethiopicum* and in particular its cultivar group "Gilo," whose small ovoid fruits range in color from red to cream; the latter are the ones that put the "egg" in eggplant. This was the first *Solanum* to be consumed in England, supplanted only later by the purple aubergine.

Though now obscure in the West, this eggplant is one of the most widely consumed vegetables in all of Africa. Several green varieties are also popular in Brazil, where it was introduced by enslaved Africans and is known as jiló, from the Kimbundu word njilu.

In Brazil, something tough to take is said to be "bitter like jiló." Indeed some types are very bitter, especially if let ripen, but others are sweet or bittersweet and may even be eaten raw. Cooked well, its flavor intensifies; it can be eaten on its own, but is also popular in a stew with mackerel and crayfish.

The garden egg is the eggplant common in the region of Lake Chad and the Chari river; this region's first inhabitants, the Sao, inspire this chant.

Chant of the Eggplant

In the region of Lake Chad,
Aubergine.
Lived a lonely giant,
Aubergine.
He liked the dancing women,
Aubergine.
Who came down from the stars,
Aubergine.
He planted white eggplant,
Aubergine.
Star women came to harvest,
Aubergine.
He captured some of them,
Aubergine.
They became his wives,
Aubergine.
Producing the first people,
Aubergine.

In the orality of the Chadic region, the original Sao—masters of clay and ceramics—
were said to be figures of gargantuan physique.

EUCALYPTUS

bahrzaf, gum tree, *Eucalyptus globulus*

It was Emperor Menelik II who first introduced eucalyptus to Ethiopia in the late 1800s. Lack of wood had long plagued the great kingdom, and tradition has it that as early as the sixteenth century an emperor brought tid trees (*Juniperus procera*) from the north to reforest the Shewa highlands. After Menelik founded Addis Ababa, there was not nearly enough wood to sustain the booming population, and this fast-growing, fragrant Australia native offered a solution. Eucalyptus would soon weave itself through the country's landscape and culture, becoming the wood of injera and folktale fire.

Eucalyptus proved a popular choice for quick afforestation in other countries too, and today it's the most widely planted tree in plantations around the world. But its utility as a timber source comes at a cost: the tree is thirsty for water, especially in spring when its sap flows, and its prodigious shedding of water-repellent leaf litter prevents the growth of other plants in its understory, leaving the soil around the trees bare and vulnerable to erosion. Using intimate knowledge of local terrain to site the trees, rather than planting in monocultures, has been shown to mitigate the worst of these effects.

In the Yoruba religion, the tree is linked to Ogun, orisha of iron.

Gebre Hanna Haiku

By eucalyptus,
As the tale goes sparkling on,
Stars spangle evening.

Aleqa Gebre Hanna, a historical figure known for his wisdom and wit, was a friend of Emperor Menelik, first importer of eucalyptus to Ethiopia. He passed into Amhara orality, becoming a central figure in their folktales. Haiku is a traditional form of Japanese poetry, consisting of three lines and seventeen syllables: five, seven, and five again. The theme of this type of poetry is the celebration of nature. I was first introduced to these writings through Basho, one of its greatest exponents; in more recent years, I've been thrilled by haiku written by Richard Wright, the African American novelist.

FIG

mugumo, *Ficus thonningii* s.l, strangler fig

The mugumo, the fig tree most sacred to Kenya's Gikuyu or Kikuyu people, is a tree of complex relationships. It often starts life as an epiphyte: the fig seed sprouts when it lands in the crevices of another tree, from which it breaks free when the roots it sends down reach the ground. At first the fig protects its host tree from storms and predators, but eventually outcompetes it (thus the name "strangler fig"); the host tree dies and the upstart, now with a hollow interior, grows to great heights.

Later in life, the fig enters into a mutualistic relationship with certain species of miniscule wasp. The queen wasp lays her eggs inside the unripe fig, actually an inside-out flower cluster that she pollinates as she lays. To sustain this helpful wasp population, the trees flower year round; hence, figs ripen at times when other food is scarce and thereby sustain wildlife of all kinds, from the bats, green pigeons, and turacos to the mammals that graze on the dropped fruits. Humans have further uses for the trees, creating shade for themselves and for their coffee crop, pounding the inner bark into barkcloth, and making medicine of the leaves and latex.

The fig tree features in the Maasai Creation Story and is the tree under which important cere-monies such as rainmaking are performed. In Yoruba religion, if someone is possessed by the orisha Shango, the leaf of this tree can cure them. When the Gikuyu God, Ngai, comes to earth, he dwells in the mugumo tree and can be reached there through ceremony and offerings; this piece recounts Ngai's first conversation with Man.

Tale of a Fig Grove

Sitting in Papine Square, Jah Folk conjured for us a picture of the fig grove of original humanity, where Gikuyu met Mumbi and the Kikuyu people began...

Sunlight comes through, dappling the glade with myriad shades of green; Gikuyu tries to count them, but gives up. The only sound is that of the birds and their ballad of joy: verses of twittering from the songbook of trills.

> Songs of the Amethyst Sunbird
> And the Lilac Roller.

And a little river runs through the sacred grove. We all know the sweet intermingling of birdsong and water melody. In light of what's come after, it's good to know that humanity came forth from a place of peace, that the first breath was called tranquility.

> Songs of the Green Honeyguide
> And the Purple Heron.

And as Gikuyu walks through the green splendor, he reflects on his conversation with God atop Mount Kenya. God telling him to go forward to yonder fig grove, where someone will be waiting for him. And as he walks, butterflies escort him, dressed in indigo and yellow; and behind them, an entourage of insects, an iridescent cavalcade.

Songs of the Emerald Cuckoo
And the Lemon Dove.

She is there waiting: destiny in the other's eyes. As they begin to love each other, the fig trees and the birds sing in unison, chanting an anthem called Kikuyu.

Songs of the Yellow Sunbird
And the Blue Turaco.

FLAME TREE

royal poinciana, flamboyan(t), peacock tree, flame of the forest, adadase, *Delonix regia*

The flame tree, a member of the bean family, is so named because of its brightly colored vermilion, orange, or yellow flowers. It has feathery foliage that looks like an acacia's and long, flat seed pods that can grow up to a foot long. These, painted red, are used as achere or maracas in the worship of Oya, the orisha of winds, storms, and the Niger River, while the tree itself belongs to the orisha of lightning, Shango.

Native to Madagascar, the flame tree is now grown throughout the tropics. On St. Martin, it is known as the July tree because the flowers reach their peak flamboyance in that month. Emancipation came to the North of the island in July of 1848, when the flame trees were in full bloom. To celebrate, St. Martiners waved the brilliant branches of the flamboyant, and the flame tree remains a national symbol.

Flame Tree Monologue

I am orange,
I am vermilion.
Take of my seedpod
When it's time to invoke her,
Bringing adimu of aubergine.

I am sunrise,
I am sunset.
I will be the sound
At the time of her calling,
With *Solanum* to lay at her shrine.

I am flame,
I am fire.
Pick and shake me for Oya,
Appealing to that orisha
With an eggplant grown just for her.

Amongst the offerings—adimu—to Oya are eggplant (aubergine), chocolate, and pomegranate. Solanum is the genus name of eggplant.

FLAME VINE

boliviana, tango, *Pyrostegia venusta*, cipó-de-são-joão, orange trumpet vine

The flame vine is a semi-woody, evergreen liana that bears dense clusters of fiery coral flowers in the form of slender trumpets, the perfect shape for a hummingbird bill. The plant is related, perhaps unsurprisingly, to the TRUMPET TREE and to the vigorous trumpet vine *Campsis radicans* of eastern North America. Flame vine is originally from South America, where it grows along highways and in fields, acting as a pioneer species in areas where trees have fallen or been removed, but its beauty soon marked it for worldwide dispersal by humans. It appears on a list of "familiar Indian flowers" in 1878 and today has naturalized in Australia, the southeastern US, and parts of east Africa.

In its native Brazil, flame vine reaches the height of its bloom in midsummer. Accordingly, it bedecks the Festas Juninas or festas de São João (the feast of St. John the Baptist, on June 24th) and derives one of its Portuguese names, cipó-de-são-joão, from this event. The leaves are used to make a popular tonic, and the Tiriyó people of Suriname extract water from the vine to treat coughs.

In the Umbanda tradition, the plant is associated with Xangô (Shango): flame vine for the orisha of fire.

Flame Vine Haiku

Brighter than humor,
The happiest of climbers
Laughs with Hummingbird.

GERANIUM

bay geranium, *Ambrosia hispida*, labsent, altamisa de playa, tapis, set vil, geranio de bahía

The bay geranium's lacy, crinkly leaves bear a passing resemblance to those of certain geraniums (and pelargoniums), but is actually a type of ragweed—as revealed by the tall green flower spikes it produces once a year. Endemic throughout the Caribbean and Central America, it is often found growing near the beach on hard-packed areas of sand behind the dunes, sometimes along with beach morning glory and BALSAM APPLE. The creeping vines perfume the seaside air with a menthol aroma and form mats that help keep the dunes stable.

On the Bahamas and other Caribbean islands, the bay geranium is an important part of the apothecary, serving as an endemic counterpart to—and sometimes sold under the name of—European herbs like wormwood and arnica. It may be made into a tea and drunk with salt and lime, or else tinctured with other herbs in rum, helping to treat colds, stomach ailments, and general malaise. It is one of the herbs added to the sacred liquid, omiero, that is used for initiation into Lukumí.

As a seaside plant, bay geranium belongs to Yemoja, orisha of the sea.

Geranium Meditation

Some have used it medicinally, others as ornament, and on an isle of the Bahamas, a woman thought of as wise used it for meditation. It was always there, ready whenever needed. The crushed leaves, interspersed with nutmeg gratings, a channel to the essence: waiting to help you, me, or anyone else who made their way to the door of Mama Farida.

After the supplicant states the problem, beginning the search for a solution, she partakes of the geranium and nutmeg mix: a sacred concoction. She goes quiet, still, like one who has lost the knowledge of movement. She goes off somewhere; where, we do not know. Maybe to speak with an ancestor, consult with someone of her calling, or hold an informal seminar with God. Soon she returns from meditation with a suggested solution.

Whatever you prefer to place in your little bowl is fine, but when it comes to easing the pain of the sufferer, Mama Farida requires a pipe filled with geranium leaves.

GESHO

mubura, shiny-leaf buckthorn,
umGlindi, *Rhamnus prinoides,*
mukarakinga

Like its relatives the buckthorns and coffeeberries of Eurasia and North America, gesho is a shrub with glossy leaves and berries. It grows along the east coast of Africa, from Ethiopia to South Africa. In Ethiopia and Eritrea, the dried and lightly roasted leaves are used to make two drinks of deep cultural importance: tej or mies (honey wine) and tella or sewa (beer). Rather like hops, gesho imparts a distinctive bitter flavor and aroma to the drink.

Farmers grow gesho in the midlands and highlands, often intercropping it with wheat or other annual crops in accordance with the ancient agroforestry practices of the region. The leaves are harvested selectively two or three times a year, while the shrubs themselves live for many decades and can grow to the height of a small house.

In southern Africa, gesho serves as a domestic talisman against lightning, like NATAL CYCAD and UMABOPHE, and also as a hunting amulet, as in this piece.

The Gesho Amulet

Across the savannah,
But how can he know?
So he's wearing a piece of gesho.

Will it be warthog or porcupine?
Maybe zebra or antelope?
Will there be safety or danger?

Deep in the forest,
Stealthy, motions slow,
He's wearing a piece of gesho.

GRAPEFRUIT

Citrus × *paradisi*, toranja, pomelo, chadèk

Citrus trees hybridize easily, even without human intervention. Most of the citrus fruits we know today are hybrids of just a handful of the original species from Asia: citron, mandarin, and pummelo. (An "×" in a scientific name is an easy way to spot a hybrid plant.) Grapefruit is such a hybrid, one among several discovered on Barbados sometime in the 18ᵗʰ century. It was found growing in the island's system of gullies: collapsed limestone caves, home to diverse flora and fauna, which once served as hidden trail networks and gathering places for the enslaved.

Apparently a backcross of a sweet orange with a pummelo, grapefruit became a favorite in Caribbean gardens and eventually spread to the American mainland. Florida was the first state to attempt commercial cultivation; grapefruit grew in such abundance in the garden of Zora Neale Hurston's childhood home there that she recalled the children using the fruit as catapult ammunition.

In Barbados, grapefruit can be eaten drizzled with Angostura bitters from nearby Trinidad; in Cuba, *dulce de toronja* is made by soaking the peel in honey. A warm-hued, luxurious fruit, it may be given to the orisha Oshun.

Grapefruit Genesis

A chant

In the beginning,
Citrus paradisi.
Could not afford a ball,
Citrus paradisi.
Used cousin of lemon,
Citrus paradisi.
Leather came later,
Citrus paradisi.
Before Santos FC,
Citrus paradisi.
"Athlete of the Century,"
Citrus paradisi.
Celebrating Pelé,
Citrus paradisi.

In the footballing traditions of Brazil, the poorer boys would often use a grapefruit to play and practice with.

GUAVA

guayaba, goyave, *Psidium guajava*, omupera, afele

Guava is native to Central and South America, where it's been cultivated since at least 2500 BCE. The name "guava" derives from *guayabo*, so named by the Taíno, the inhabitants of Haiti who first introduced Europeans to the fruit. Today, guavas grow throughout the world; India produces nearly half the world's crop, while in Hawai'i the strawberry guava has become both a fixture of local cuisine and a pernicious weed.

The guava, a beautiful tree as well as a useful one, exfoliates itself as it grows, shedding silvery outer bark to reveal a new reddish layer underneath. The yellow-green fruit is often a striking salmon color inside. Goiabada or guava cheese, sliceable jelly, is popular in Brazil and the Caribbean, as are guava-filled pastelitos or puff pastries. In southern Africa the fruits are made into wine. The fruit is rich in vitamins and minerals, and the other parts of the plant have healing properties as well; the buds can be chewed for stomachache, and the young stems make good toothbrushes.

In Taíno belief, the spirits of the deceased, called opias or jupias, come out at night as bats to feed on guavas. The Taíno zemí or spirit who rules the underworld, Maquetaurie Guayaba, has guava as part of his name.

Guava is one of the offerings that can be given to Elegua, orisha of crossroads and messages. Elegua's staff or *garabato* is made of guava wood; with it he opens and closes the gateways of life.

Tale of Guava

As soon as he said the words guava jelly, the whole place erupted, gently. Some started humming the melody with that sweet lead guitar while others sang the refrain: "Here I am/ Come rub it 'pon me belly like guava jelly." Then they sang it through again. It lasted just a few moments, and afterward, everyone was laughing, grinning and touching fists. Just a few moments, but at times like that, there's nowhere else I'd rather be than there in Papine Square.

Then, Jah Folk told us of Orisha, of the Yoruba and a connection to guava. He took us first to Ife in Nigeria, where the Yoruba believe humanity began—Ife, where they produced magnificence in terracotta, ivory, brass, and wood—and then from the sacred city, across the Atlantic, to the places of ceremonies throughout the Americas. For belief had come with the enslaved, to Trinidad, Brazil, and Cuba. He recited a poem, entitled "Yoruba," which I learned by heart over the following days:

Enslaved boy thrown overboard: another Black cadaver,
in the
Atlantic cemetery. But he remains—he lives.
For they wanted manpower, but his fellow captives
brought God power too. On the beach in Bahia,

they celebrate Yemoja.
Yoruba, Yoruba.

Let's take a journey then, you and I,
Through Brazil and Venezuela,
To see and hear Macumba.
Yoruba, Yoruba.

Into Mexico and Panama,
Honoring the orishas.
Yoruba, Yoruba.

Uruguay and Argentina,
Olorun and Oduduwa.
Yoruba, Yoruba.

Puerto Rico and Cuba,
To experience Santería.
Yoruba, Yoruba.

Let's go to Brazil, you and I,
To the beach in Bahia.
The Festival of Goddess Yemoja.
Yoruba, Yoruba.

Some of us had heard of the Yoruba, but he took us deeper, talking of the orishas, the deities of all we need, such as rivers, love, guidance, and trees. And each deity receives items of flora: designated fruit, vegetables, or herbs as offerings in the shrines and *terreiros*. For example, to Oku, orisha of agriculture, you can offer sweet potato; for Yemoja, an orisha of rivers, amongst the things you can bring her is watermelon.

Then a discussion ensued—after he explained about the ritual preparation of offerings—about the way we'd offer it. There were votes for pudding, soup, crisps, and fries. It should be roasted! Preference for grilled! And when we got to talking about making sweet potato pudding, that was it! Most wanted raisins; a few didn't. Some went for more butter, others coconut milk. Cinnamon or ginger? Nutmeg or allspice? And so it went. The cooking of sweet potato had never been dissected like how it was on that Papine evening.

Then, informing us he had a lecture to deliver the following morning, he deferred further examination of sweet potato pudding until a later time. He concluded by introducing us to the orisha of pathways: of roads, crossroads, and destinies. Guardian of the gate, opener and closer of doors, the one called Elegua. And one of the items offered to Elegua is guava.

As we dispersed, here and there, I could hear snippets of the melody and words of that Bob Marley song, "Guava Jelly."

HELICONIA

Heliconia bihai, balisier, macawflower, lobster-claw, red palulu, bijao, bananeira do mato, platanillo

Heliconia is a plant with bright, dramatic flowers native to the tropical regions of the Americas. As some of its names reflect, it is a relative of cannas as well as bananas and plantains. Heliconia are grown ornamentally for their ornate flowers, which take the form of many staggered, cup-like extensions on a single flower spike. They also grow in the wild, in forest clearings. In that setting, their bracts often fill with water and provide a habitat to various insect species, including mosquitoes. Because of their role in sustaining insect populations, heliconia are regarded as a keystone species to the tropical forest ecologies of the New World.

The banana-like leaves of the heliconia are used as tamale wrappers in some parts of Mexico where the plant grows wild. In Martinique, the heliconia flower is a symbol of the Progressive Party, chosen by the poet Aimé Césaire, the party's founder.

New World heliconias are almost all pollinated by hummingbirds. Heliconia and hummingbirds have evolved together over millions of years, and many heliconia species are specially adapted for particular types of hummingbird. In Jamaica, two different heliconia species have adapted to the differently-sized male and female of a single hummingbird species. This serenade honors the partnership of bird and flower.

Heliconia Serenade

Listen. If it is true that there is a time and a place for everything under the sun, then now is the time to listen. Listen; and you will hear Hummingbird giving thanks to Heliconia for the everyday blessings she offers. Tomorrow, we may hear the conversation between the two butterflies, bubbling between the banana trees; but today, we'll speak of the one who goes purple spangling through the green splendor. And during the thanksgiving, the reverence generates song. Tell me, did you ever hear a hummingbird sing?

> "I could sing for the flame tree,
> On its vermilion raid.
> I could sing for the grass,
> Each and every blade.
> But I'll sing for you,
> I know what is due:
> Please accept this serenade."

Their interaction is long, of benefit to both, in the Garden of Beautiful Symbiosis. Like the Sugar Minott classic, "I've Got A Good Thing Going," Hummingbird knows he's blessed, so he happily sings of her. Because of the deep

respect between them—he's continually in her presence—
he's become known as the Guardian of Heliconia.

> "I could sing for citrus
> Generating lemonade.
> I could sing for bougainvillea,
> And its rainbow parade.
> But I'll sing for you,
> Your tricolor hue:
> Please accept this serenade."

Who better to watch over her than the one who admires
her most deeply. In their years of intermingling there has
never been commotion, as respect meanders through every
thought and action. Like the egret and the cow, they work
well together, an exemplary partnership. Listen, so you can
hear the Heliconia Serenade.

> "I could sing for the vines,
> Those resembling hair braids.
> I could sing for *Artocarpus*,
> From the breadfruit glade.
> But I'll sing for you,
> I don't need a cue:
> Please accept this serenade."

HIBISCUS

sorrel, roselle, *Hibiscus sabdariffa*, cuxá, isapa, flor de jamaica, bissap, caruru-azedo, quiabo-azedo

The hibiscus species that is used to make sorrel is notable for its crepey flower but also for the fleshy cranberry-red calyx at its base, which shows the plant's family connection to okra. These fruits are brewed into the tart, refreshing drink, known variously as bissap, zobo, and zobolo in West Africa, vinagreira in Brazil, and agua de Jamaica in Latin America.

As the latter name might suggest, the plant and the beverage are inextricably linked with the Caribbean, but roselle was originally from Africa, where it has many uses besides the beverage: the plant's leaves are used to make miyan taushe, a savory Nigerian pumpkin dish, and the seeds are fermented into a fish-sauce-like condiment, datu.

Roselle and other hibiscus species came to the New World with enslaved Africans, who grew them for sorrel and as a medicinal plant in their provision grounds. Later, they were a staple plant in "Creole gardens," biodiverse, multistory backyard mini-farms.

In the US, sorrel or red drink is a Juneteenth tradition, along with other red foods. The color is associated with liberty and struggle throughout the Caribbean (see FLAME TREE) and with West African ceremony via the kola nut, which also has a red juice. Hibiscus is the national flower of Haiti, but poets from Aimé Césaire to Kendel Hippolyte have used it as an emblem of the violence in the island's history as well.

Tale of Sorrel

Jah Folk began by asking, "What is your favorite drink,
after water, to quench thirst on the hottest of days?" Some
said coconut water, others said ginger beer, and some said
sorrel. And with the mention of the latter, he told us in
verse—with us chanting "Anansi"—the story of the coming
of sorrel drink:

> He goes strolling along,
>> Anansi.
> He sees some red stalks,
>> Anansi.
> Doesn't know what they are,
>> Anansi.
> Still, he picks a few,
>> Anansi.
> Takes them to market,
>> Anansi.
> A misunderstanding,
>> Anansi.
> Chased by a vendor,
>> Anansi.
> Throws away the stalks,
>> Anansi.

In a pot of hot water,
Anansi.
People love the color,
Anansi.
And the aroma,
Anansi.
He suggests cinnamon,
Anansi.
A sprinkling of ginger,
Anansi.
He gets all the credit,
Anansi.
Inventor of sorrel drink,
Anansi.

After the verse, there began a discussion of what Tommy and I called "Anansi drink." Cinnamon and ginger? How much orange peel? Which kinds of berries? How much sugar? Maybe cloves? Jah Folk sat back and smiled as those stationary and those passing by spoke of the hibiscus elixir.

IBHULU

imfenyane, ruikbossie, *Senecio rhyncholaenus,* mahoaneng

Ibhulu is a shrub in the huge polyphyletic genus *Senecio*. It has ferny, finely cut leaves, which are sticky and sweetly scented—hence its Afrikaans name *ruikbossie*, "smelly bush." Its flowers come in branching clusters and are shaped like tiny half-open dandelions, cream in color. It is one of the many plants endemic to the biodiversity hotspot comprising Maputaland and Pondoland in eastern South Africa and Eswatini, where ibhulu grows on rocky outcrops, often near the coast.

The Basotho traditionally inhale the smoke of ibhulu to relieve colds and they make a tea from the plant's roots, while Zulu people use it for blackening pottery, heating it, then rubbing it on the pot after firing.

For the amaMpondo of Pondoland, it is a talismanic plant, much like the umguza (NATAL CYCAD). Its uses in the Pondoland, which include preventing and treating lightning strikes (often in conjunction with UMABOPHE) and helping nursing mothers, are the subject of this chant.

Ibhulu

Ibhulu, ibhulu,
Sit on leaves of ibhulu,
You who are nursing a child.
Ibhulu, Ibhulu,
Imbibe imbhulu:
Alleviation of pressure.
Ibhulu, ibhulu,
Burn some ibhulu,
Counteracting lightning.

IROKO

Milicia excelsa, oji, uloho, odum

The iroko tree is a close relative of mulberry that grows all along the west coast of Africa where rainfall conditions allow. Healers use its leaves and bark to treat headaches, fevers, and many other maladies. Iroko wood also has unique properties that make it well-suited for building in tropical regions: it's strong, it resists rot, and it even holds up against termites.

The wood's durability and warm coppery color have created an international market for iroko, and wild populations have been heavily logged. Many iroko trees have survived on farms or in villages, preserved by those who regard the trees as sacred to divinities like Loko, or under the protection of dangerous spirits like the Iroko Man of this piece, who may become trapped in furniture made of the wood. To take leaves, bark, or wood from these trees, villagers need to enter into negotiations with religious specialists who protect the iroko from overexploitation. Yet these sacred connections have also turned to the tree's disadvantage, since many iroko trees were destroyed during an "anti-witchcraft" campaign carried out by the government of Benin in the 1970s.

Iroko is an orisha in his own right, the patron of roots, ancestry, and time. In Brazil, he may be worshiped by way of the closely related gameleira tree (*Ficus gomelleira*) or other *Ficus* species. In the Caribbean, this orisha is often associated with the KAPOK.

Iroko Man

I heard you crying last night, Iroko Man. Coming out from the shelving, a heavy chant from an unknown place.

Taken from your forest to our city, your spirit trapped within the wood. Forced to leave the meditative and thrown into noise. You can no longer wander near the trees of your name, watching over them day and night. All your sunsets and sunrises are muted now; the brilliance of celestial masterpiece is dimmed.

I heard you singing of displacement, and for a moment, I wanted to accompany you with drum, but your song captivated me; I shed a quiet tear, listening to your yearning for home.

For all the refugees

JACKALBERRY

nelbi, *Diospyros mespiliformis*, igi dúdu, onye oji, monkey guava, African ebony, omwandi

The jackalberry tree, treasured through much of Africa, is closely related to both persimmon and true ebony (*D. ebenum.*) Its small, downy fruits, which range in color from yellow to dark purple-brown when ripe, resemble persimmon, sharing that fruit's chalkiness if underripe. The fruits have long been used to brew local beers, as is the American persimmon in the US South, in a tradition perhaps inaugurated by enslaved Africans preserving ancestral foodways.

The tree, like the TAMARIND and some species of FIG, has a special affinity for the great termite mounds that dot the African savanna. Growing on such mounds, the jackalberry acts as a "mother tree," its roots housing snakes and other critters. The mounds make excellent fire breaks and allow the soil to drain well, while the termites themselves break down leaf litter, increasing soil fertility. Monkeys and jackals enjoy the tree's fruits, while elephants and other large mammals browse on the leaves.

In Namibia, the fruit is one of the ingredients in ombike, the traditional hot liquor of the Owambo people, and the pounded fruits are also mixed with millet meal to make oshihenyandi, a much-loved porridge, . Jackalberry wood is also used to craft the dugout canoes called morokos popular on Botswana's rivers. The Wolof, the Makua, and the Fula featured in this piece all employ the roots to ward off bad magic; the tree itself, to the Fula and to other peoples, is viewed as sacred, the home of spirits and ancestors.

Tribute to Nelbi

Only one tree will do. Since time immemorial, from that tree has come our tool for walking, prodding and first defense. So let me, man of the Peul, also known as Fulani, chant of the tree we call Nelbi.

> Fulani man chanting
> Of flora that is sacred to us.
> Some call it Monkey Guava
> Or African Ebony;
> I chant a tribute to Nelbi.

Like my ancestors who crossed the savannas from Senegal to Sudan, appareled in blue, conical-hatted, I watch over the ones central to my life.

> Fulani man chanting
> Of flora that is sacred to us.
> Some call it Mokochong
> Or Jackal Berry;
> I chant a tribute to Nelbi.

Could you, the best of staffs, fight off the bringer of Armageddon? Could I use it to defend myself from the most feared of all the witches, Njeddo Dewal, the courier

of final catastrophe?

> Fulani man chanting
> Of flora that is sacred to us.
> Some call it Zalama
> Or Omwandi;
> I chant a tribute to Nelbi.

As well as excelling at animal husbandry, the Fulani have produced some of the greatest scholars of the continent, such as Muhammed Bello, Nana Asma'u, Muhammed al- Fulani al-Kishnawi and Muhammed al-Kaburi, a pioneering scholar of Timbuktu University. For more on these figures, see TAMARIND.

Njeddo Dewal is the arch-witch of Fulani orality. Possessing three eyes and seven ears, she is known as "Mother of Calamity," destroyer of the mythical country called Heli and Yoyo, where tranquility permeated every day. I first came across her in excerpts from Contes Initiatiques Peuls (Fulani Initiation Stories) by the Fulani scholar Amadou Hampâté Bâ.

JATOBA

stinking toe, *Hymenaea courbaril,*
guapinol, West Indian locust

The jatoba is a tree in the legume family *Fabaceae*, and it produces fruit that comes in the form of large beanlike seedpods, like its relatives ACACIA, FLAME TREE and TAMARIND. The jatoba's seedpods are stubby, tough, and bulbous, like the toe of a giant, and the powdery flesh inside it is edible but smelly–hence the fruit's name in the Caribbean, "stinking toe."

The tree is native to Brazil and was dispersed through much of South America and into the Caribbean in part by elephant-like mammals called gomphoth-eres, who ate and excreted the seeds. Now that they're extinct, the tree survives thanks to the agouti, a rodent known for its scatter-hoarding behavior: fond of the jatoba's large seeds, it caches them, then repeatedly digs them up and caches them again, ulti-mately moving them hundreds of yards away from their initial location. The jatoba is one of the largest trees in the Caribbean, forming the upper part of the canopy in rainforests and living for hundreds of years.

For humans, the dry "pulp" that surrounds the seeds is both nutri-tious and, if you can get past the smell, delicious; it can be crumbled into a kind of flour and used in baked goods, or blended with nutmeg and sugar into juice. The tree itself is one of Brazil's most valuable timber species, known as "Brazilian cherry" because of its reddish-brown heartwood, and it is often the target of illegal logging. The tree also produces a copal or resin that matures into amber (Domincan amber comes from jatoba's extinct sibling, *H. protera*) and has many medicinal and wound-healing properties, utilized by Buzzard in this piece.

Tale of Stinking Toe

Jah Folk told us another story from Brazil, reminding us that we shouldn't be too quick to follow the next man, attempting to emulate him. The reminder came through a story in which the jatoba tree, which we call Stinking Toe, plays a central role. What worked for Crab didn't work for Jaguar. So then we spoke of the consequences of envy: religious sects, political discipleship; of the young hustler, following the older gangster.

To finish that evening in Papine Square, which became known as "Boomerang Night," Jah Folk recited this poem, saying, "Watch what you do and what comes back to you."

> Did you ever see a crab play boomerang,
> Across Lake Palana where tilapia sang?
> Did you ever see such a thing?
>
> Sent his eyes across the water;
> Their return met with laughter,
> Conjuring Crustacea magic.
>
> Jaguar yearned to join in,
> Though Crab gave a warning,
> Of little fish with sharpest teeth.
>
> Removed from their sockets,

Sent them off like rockets,
But his eyeballs did not return.

So Jaguar lost eyesight,
Entangled in night,
As darkness invaded his world.

Then came Buzzard his neighbor
In the role of the savior,
Bringing sap from Jatoba tree.

Put the sap in the holes,
Dark as coals,
Then washed them with water that's fresh.

Buzzard saved the day;
Victim vowed never to play
That game of eye boomerang.

Gave thanks to his savior
For Jatoba elixir,
Conquering visual impairment.

KAPOK

silk cotton, araba, mapou, *Ceiba pentandra,* yaxche, kumaka

Kapok is a Malay word used to refer to a number of different trees that produce fine, cotton-like fiber. The main kapok that grows in America, Africa, and the Caribbean is ceiba, *Ceiba pentandra,* a very tall tree with distinctive buttressing roots, spines along its trunk, and branches that produces cream-colored flowers. These develop into seed pods stuffed full of the aforementioned fiber, which has been used for everything from blowgun darts to life vests. Ceiba is unusual in having grown in both Africa and America since long before humans crossed the Atlantic.

Before the Spanish conquest, ceiba was sacred to the Maya, who identified it with the green tree at the center of the world. West African farmers probably bred the modern domestic ceiba, which is a hybrid of Caribbean and Guinean varieties and produces seed pods that stay closed rather than splitting open and casting their precious fiber to the winds. But even domesticated, the pods are difficult to harvest; workers must still split the pods and separate out the fiber by hand.

Practitioners identify ceiba with IROKO, a ritually important tree that grows on the west coast of Africa, and it hosts the Iroko orisha along with Ogun, Oko, and a number of others. People who want to ask the aid of these orishas leave offerings at the feet of ceiba trees, and people who want to cut the trees down take care to propitiate the spirits they contain.

Tale of Silk Cotton

You used a horn,
Spearing my auntie,
But you can't kill me.

Utilized your four hooves,
Trampling brother Kwesi,
But you can't kill me.

You think you're invincible, Gashanami.
So let me tell you,
I am the fearless one:
You cannot kill me.

So sang a young man from a silk cotton tree, taunting, incensed at the carnage of the dreaded bull and its calves rampaging through his village. They had charged down from that part of Kingston we now know as Gordon Town into Papine, ferrying devastation: Hurricane Gashanami. From the square in Gordon Town where the statue of Miss Lou stands to the square in Papine where a few vendors sit alongside the watchers of the world going by, they came storm-trooping through, mashing down trees and houses. It was a time when the soil sang "Uprooted Blues," The mango sang a verse of early removal, and the blossom of the flame tree cried a cascade of orange.

In other parts of the city, people began to board up and barricade their homes in case the bovine regiment came stomping through. And you know how it is with all the stories about shapeshifting. Here and there, people began to see things, hallucinate, lose consciousness, or bring down damnation on the rest of the community. As well as physical destruction, there was also damage to the mind.

And the young man Kwame can't rid his mind of the death of Afia, killed by the hated bull while she was washing clothes in Hope River. Everyone loved her. She was the unofficial princess of the village because she was gentle and generous to all. In many cases, I think her death affected some mourners more than their personal losses. Young and old loved to be in her company; she was almost like a talisman to them, a little totem; the elders called her the Cherished One.

What would you use in your defense? What item would you choose as your bulwark against the bull? Our emerging hero chose a silk cotton tree, as have many others down through the ages. For the Caribs, when they descended from their home on the moon, it was the tree of survival—bearing all kinds of fruit in the time of famine—during their first residence on Earth.

In one of the great stories of the Hausa, Zankallala, who is escorted always by birds who sing of him, uses one of these trees to hide a boy from the monster Dodo, who is chasing him for food. And Ozidi, the hero of the eponymous epic of the Ijo, uproots a silk cotton tree to bring firewood to his mother! So Kwame, from his chosen bastion against the bull, challenges him in song. And as you can imagine, the taunting enrages the bull. He begins to charge, using himself like the battering ram of medieval times. And with each charge, he grows bigger—like the guy going back and forth to prison—and the tree begins to bend.

So Kwame sings another song:

> This is no time to falter,
> To stumble and fall:
> Raise your head, silk cotton tree.
> I need you,
> We need you:
> Help me end our misery.
>
> This is no time to bend,
> To stagger and drop:
> Raise your head, silk cotton tree.
> Hear my plea,
> Our request,
> Help me kill monstrosity.

The tree appears to listen to the chant. It straightens up, and before long the bull begins to tire. Battling with a silk cotton tree isn't like the momentary skirmish with a banana tree! He's got all those buttresses to deal with, as well as the main body. I wonder, did his hooves sometimes slip on those massive roots? Did a horn get stuck in the trunk? They battled on for two days, through the firefly nights and the John Crow afternoons. After two days of battle, Gashanami, exhausted, fell. The prison bully can't batter the prison wall. With an axe, Kwame finishes him off.

Anyway, Gashanami should have known better than to mess with a silk cotton tree! Its name might not sound like much, but it's one of the trees I wouldn't tangle with—the other three being the baobab, iroko, and fig. You're never going to defeat those buttress brigades!

So after lamentation, people sang. No longer would their homes, of whatever material, be susceptible to such an onslaught. Their ackee and jackfruit trees would now be safe from attack worse than canker and blight.

All over Gordon Town and Papine, people sang, like at the Homowo Festival in ancestral Ghana, where the Ga people hoot at hunger after surviving famine; so the people in that part of Jamaica jeered at the passing of their nemesis. They sang two songs: one for an old tree known as silk cotton and one for a young man called Kwame.

And while the people sang, Kwame went down by Hope River, reflecting and giving thanks. Giving thanks for rescue and for the blessings that can still be counted. Giving thanks, as the Caribs did, to Kabo Tano, the Creator. He knows there will be a commemoration annually on this day of deliverance. But now, while the sun plays her glinting melody on the water, he sits in the shade of other trees, writing the first part of a song of eternal gratitude:

> I could kiss a butterfly,
> Dance with a hummingbird,
> Write a poem for coconut water,
> Ballad for bougainvillea.
> And I'll continue writing

Anthem for a Silk Cotton Tree.

Friendship bracelet for tody,
Luncheon date with oriole.
Blessings from cold sorrel,
Benediction of ginger.
I'll be composing always
Anthem for a Silk Cotton Tree.

For David Brailsford and Sharon Barcan Elswit.

In my transcription of this tale, I've kept the three central aspects—bull, hero, and tree—but added verse and changed the location and name of the hero.

A John Crow is a turkey vulture; a tody is a tiny Caribbean bird with brilliant multicolored plumage.

LEMON

Citrus × *limon*, lomi, sitwon

Citrus fruits grow on short, sometimes thorny, evergreen trees notable for their nearly year-round flowering. They originated in the Himalayan foothills and moved eastward to China, Southeast Asia, and Australia, where people began to domesticate them. Lemons were consumed in the Roman Empire as an elite product, but were not grown widely in Europe until North Africans introduced them to Spain, along with superior irrigation systems, during the Umayyad Caliphate.

In the 12ᵗʰ century, the Egyptian Jewish physician Ibn Jumay' wrote a treatise on the dietetic value of lemons, including recipes for preserved lemons—still an essential condiment in North African cookery—and lemonade. The leaves of lemons and limes were well known as a remedy throughout Africa. Columbus brought lemon seeds to the Caribbean in 1493, and lemons were also carried on slave ships.

Adding lemon or lime to barbecue sauce is a Florida tradition with its origins in West and Central Africa, and lemon ice box pie is a Southern Thanksgiving tradition alongside sweet potato pie. The lemon's power as a gris-gris, or charm, is also believed to repel spirits in the Caribbean Islands and can account for the practice of planting lime trees in the church yards of Antigua.

Interlude of Lemons

One enthused,
Spoke of lemon and lime marmalade.
Another of lemon juice,
For sardine marinade:
When I mentioned the Timkat celebrations.

Someone said chili and ginger
for making a lemon pickle.
Another suggested its juice
in a recipe for baked apple
From my introducing Timkat in Ethiopia.

You see, in a country that accepted Christianity in the fourth
century, Timkat is one of the major commemorations of the
baptism of Jesus. The imperial city of Gondar is a famed
location for this annual celebration, taking place around
and in Fasilides Pool, named after the seventeenth-century
emperor who built the city. And now, you're thinking to
yourself, "What has this got to do with lemons?" In the
first country to depict a Christian symbol—a cross—on its
coinage, what is the connection to *Citrus limon*?

Well, during this time of enhanced spirituality, there is

a romantic interlude. Young people gather together and form two lines: one for young women, the other for their male peers. The latter hold a lemon in their hands, which they throw across the room to the female they're attracted to. If the attraction is shared, she catches the yellow item; if it isn't mutual, she purposely drops it. Imagine the level of excitement, apprehension, and aftermath of disappointment! The genesis of marriage for some could be the divorce of attraction for others after the yellow projectile, accompanied by a smile, is sent with a prayer and best wishes:

I'd never heard
Of a lemon, yogurt, and oatmeal muffin.
Or of pancakes
With lemon, banana, and honey filling:
All from talking of Timkat.

Someone suggested
Lemon and garlic chicken.
Another said lemon and dill
When preparing roasted salmon,
Concluding our talk of Timkat.

LEMONGRASS

mchaichai, *Cymbopogon citratus*, koriko oba, yerba de limón, caña santa, capim-cidreira, capim-santo, eti, ewe tea

As its name suggests, lemongrass is a thick-stemmed, citrus-scented grass that grows in thick, tall tussocks. It's a close relative of a lot of other food crops, including corn, sugarcane, and millet. Lemongrass spread from Southern India to the east coast of Africa thousands of years ago, probably as a result of the "monsoon trade" that linked the continents during the rainy season. The plant grows quickly in tropical areas and can be invasive, but lemongrass, like many other grasses, can play a positive role in stabilizing dunes or soils prone to flooding.

In Africa and the Caribbean, lemongrass is not just an herb but also a medicine. An infusion, known in Nigeria simply as "leaf tea," is drunk to boost immunity and as an ingredient in other bitter tonics. Maroon communities in the Caribbean used lemongrass to treat respiratory ailments. In Haiti, lemongrass flavors the drink known as tifey which is made by macerating it in sugarcane spirits. The scent of lemongrass can repel mosquitoes, and it is the source of citronella oil, along with other *Cymbopogon* species—but it actually attracts other kinds of insects, including bees. Either way, it's a fragrance the insects in this story would have noticed!

Tale of Lemongrass

Walking past Tastee's, Jah Folk bought a tube of incense from another Ras elder passing through Papine. And by the time he got to the square and lit a stick, he had changed the story in his head to the one about Sadaka. While lemongrass—which we call fever grass—meandered amongst us, he told a tale of generosity and the reality of karma. A tale told by the Swahili who traded frankincense and gold across the Indian Ocean.

So this Sadaka, a gentle soul, is traversing the lands in search of his long-lost brothers. On his way, on three occasions, he shares what he has with those in need: with birds, spirits, and insects. And after each encounter, as a token of gratitude, each group gives him something he can signal to them with if ever he's in danger: an incense stick.

Jah Folk's telling of this story produced what became known as the Aromatic Debate, as most of those gathered in the square expressed a personal preference. I heard votes for cinnamon. A couple said lavender. Someone stated that sage is good for easing off pressure; another, that rosemary is an aid to concentration. And so it went: tangerine, sandalwood, musk... Jah Folk said his favorite was coconut and mango: the sweetest combination. And with that he returned us to the story, where our hero is entangled in a dilemma. For a chance of marrying the prin-cess, the standard reward in episodes of challenge featuring a young woman—no courting, just the ceremony—he has to surmount three of the highest hurdles ever set; one is the felling of a baobab tree. After brainstorm and headache, he thinks of the insects. Lighting a stick of the incense they'd given him, he summons them to his aid. They gnaw through the tree unseen, before the spectators gather; later, in front of everyone, with one chop of Sadaka's, the tree falls.

The question of what he'd lit to call his new friends set off Aromatic Debate Part Two, as people voiced their opinions about the fragrance of SOS: patchouli, jasmine, cherry, rose... From then until now, whenever I've heard the word "lemongrass" or seen it somewhere, my first thought is always of that evening in the square when we spoke about aroma.

In addition to Sadaka, the hero, other characters the Swahili have given us include Sebgugugu, the glutton; Sungara, the trickster hare; and Segu, the honeyguide.

LIANA

"Liana" is a general term for a vine whose stem is woody, like that of a tree or shrub. We have met two already in these pages: BOUGAIN-VILLEA and FLAME VINE. Lianas abound in tropical rainforests, but they grow in temperate regions as well: poison ivy, Virginia creeper, wisteria, grape, and kudzu are all lianas. Some plants, including relatives of CASSAVA in the *Manihot* genus, may take the form of a liana under certain conditions but not under others.

As humans disturb the forests and the planet warms, lianas thrive, increasing in abundance, density, and size, for reasons scien-tists are still working to under-stand. All climbing plants rely on sturdy-trunked trees to reach the light they need; lianas, with their thick, strong stems, often achieve this goal at the expense of their hosts. Because lianas outcompete trees, particularly timber crops growing in previously logged areas, and sequester less carbon than their non-climbing coun-terparts, liana removal has lately been touted as a "cost-effective climate solution." But the ecolog-ical interplay of lianas, trees, and other forest dwellers is complex, varying considerably from one forest to another. A liana might threaten a tree, but it might also shield a delicate sapling from fire, make a road for a sloth, provide food for an ape—or foil a greedy human, as in this piece.

The Liana Declaration

Some call me Vine,
Others Liana.
I work with Papa Bwa,
Confusing the hunter,
Making them trip and fall,
Listening as they call,
"Help me."

I entangle
The forest offender,
That man of excess,
Unwanted visitor.
Watching him stumble,
Groan and then grumble,
I assist Agouti.

Papa Bwa is the guardian of the forest in Trinidadian folklore: half man, half goat.
He carries a flute—in some versions a bell—to warn the animals of incoming danger.
"Bwa" comes from the French word "bois," wood.
   The agouti is a rodent, the quarry of the hunter.

MALLOW

malva de caballo, *Malachra capitata*,
herbe à balais, ti-lalo

Growing all over Cuba can be found a group of inconspicuous, weedy plants in the mallow family with small yellow flowers, almost primrose-like at first glance, but bearing five petals around the same columnar stamens as their cousins okra and hibiscus.

Although a tourist might easily overlook the mallow, those knowledgeable about plants throughout the Caribbean put it to good use. Its bitter root is used with ginger against fever; some add it to cocktails; and in Cuban Vodou it is part of the mourning ritual. In Haiti it wards off malevolent spirits and people. It might also feature in the Cuban equivalent of Roots Tonic, the herbal mixtures known as galones. (See CHANEY ROOT.)

The stem of the plant, like that of many of its relatives (especially *Sida rhombifolia*), contain a strong fiber, long used to make rope. Perhaps that is why the plant is good for keeping a monster in its place.

The Mallow Grave

You may not have heard of me, but my cousin may be familiar to you. He's probably the most well-known member of our family: the one you call Hibiscus or Sorrel.

One thing I'm known for, though, in Cuba, is my part in the demise of Okurri Boroku, the demonic one—the square-faced, two-toned one—who has the longest, sharpest teeth known to flora, fauna, and man.

For the one of quadrilateral visage had placed a curse on the whole island: the curse of lostness. Although people knew where they were, they felt somewhat lost. You see, all the roads and pathways had vanished, as if Eshu had withdrawn from the world. And a high, seemingly endless forest had appeared, enshrouding all, blocking everything. Restlessness and loneliness set in, as no one could visit their beloved ones or go to market in the next village. Those who ventured into the green shroud were never seen again.

The twins Taiwo and Kehinde, trapped in disquietude, decide to leave the village to see what lies beyond the shroud. On their way—in fact, blocking their way—is the gargantuan one, lying on the beach in sharp-faced sleep. Taiwo speaks with him first and accepts the bet: who can outlast the other? The monster, dancing, or the youth, playing the guitar? But unbeknownst to the member of the ogre fraternity, there is someone who looks just like Taiwo! So as one twin tires, when their adversary isn't looking, the other takes his place, wearing out the feet and the spirit of Square Jaw; eventually, he falls.

Then, the ebony talisman that each one wears instructs them to remove his heart, cut it up, and mash it with my leaves, to be placed in a clay pot and buried in the forest.

No, you may not know my name, but I am part of the final tale of Okurri Boroku. He shall not rise again, for he's buried in a mallow grave.

African and Caribbean folklore have a distinctive bestiary. There's the axe-headed Bulgu of the Oromo of Ethiopia; Chiruwi—half flesh, half wax—of the Chewa of Malawi; Makhanda Mahlanu of the five heads of the Zulu of South Africa; and the iron-toothed, iron-footed Sasabonsam of the Ashanti of Ghana, to name a few. Eshu (also known as Elegua—see RASPBERRY) is the Yoruba orisha of gateways roads and messages.

MANGO

Mangifera indica, oro, eleso

Mangos are the fruit of a tall, long-lived tree that originated in tropical South Asia and was introduced to Africa in the Middle Ages by Islamic traders; the tree called "wild mango" in Africa is not related. Portuguese colonists later carried mangos to Brazil, whence they spread to Mexico and the Caribbean. There are over 400 varieties of mango, with fruits that differ in color, texture, and flavor. At the heart of the mango fruit is a kernel which can be squeezed for the oil out of which mango butter is made.

The mango is a popular urban tree in Africa and the Caribbean. It is also grown on plantations in Mexico and elsewhere in South and Central America. Alongside lemongrass, mangos are one of the most widely used plant medicines in the Caribbean—not only the fruits, but also the flowers, which are made into a tea for treating stomach ulcers. In Vodou, mango trees are the repozwa or dwelling place of Sen Jak Majè and the Marasa. The fruits are associated with the orisha Ogun and with Ibeji, orisha of twins.

The Mango Juggler

The Mango Juggler always wore yellow and green and only appeared on one day of the year: September 7th, the birthday of Miss Lou. Where he came from, no one knows, and where he went to after the performance, we were equally ignorant. He came, performed, and went. Everyone would gather round her statute in Gordon Town Square, and amongst the tributes and candles, Mango Juggler would perform. Whereas other jugglers might have found the mango too heavy, he said he liked the shape of the fruit, as if his hands had been molded to hold and catch it. It seemed like the Goddess of *Mangifera* had personally blessed his hands. He would juggle, and as he manipulated the rise and fall, he'd chant of his favorite fruit.

I remember when Jah Folk told that story, generating a discussion about the medicinal benefits of mango, telling us of Liliane Nérette Louis, a Haitian storyteller and traditional healer. People coming to buy pineapple, mango, ackee, or coconut water joined in the discussion. The pavement became a place of joyful opinion as well as daily trudging. As laughter weaved its way amongst the fruit and conversation, we spoke of festivals too: mango festivals in India, yam festivities in Ghana, and ackee festivals in Jamaica.

And Jah Folk led us in the Mango Juggler's chant; we joined in for the last line, with "Man-go." We sang it through twice, as the assembled began to take over the path and the curbside of the road, people having to step out into the traffic to pass by, or to listen and join in:

> Can I take a leaf or two,
> For the diabetes sufferer:
> Mango.
>
> You assist the leaf doctor,
> The one called Mama Liliane:
> Mango.
>
> Born and raised in Asia,
> Now you bless the whole world:
> Mango.
>
> Giving thanks for the healing,
> The sweetest generosity:
> Mango.

Louise Bennett, a.k.a. Miss Lou, is the iconic figure of Jamaican folklore, born in Gordon Town, up the road from Papine. Now resident in America, Lilian Nérette Louis is a Haitian storyteller, cook—her pumpkin soup is said to be legendary—and leaf doctor.

In a tale from Trinidad, "How The Hunter Poisoned The Mango Tree," a hunter is saved by the sacrifice of the tree. The fruit is also featured in a story of the Fon from Benin, "The Name Guessing Contest."

MILLET

*bede, mwele, maiwa, ngma,
Pennisetum glaucum

"Millet" can refer to a number of more or less closely related grasses that bear heads full of small, nutritious seeds. Some varieties, like pearl millet and finger millet, are named in a way that gives you an idea what they look like.

Millet has been part of the human diet for thousands of years. Finger millet was first domesticated in East Africa, and pearl millet was domesticated in West Africa. Both crops give good harvests on poor soils and without much water input, and they can be used as animal forage in addition to providing a reliable food source for human beings.

Millet was brought to the Caribbean in the 17th century by enslaved Africans, who grew it in provision grounds. Alongside sorghum, sweet potato, and plantain, millet was one of the main crops grown by Maroon communities of people who had escaped from slavery. It is still an important part of Caribbean cuisine today, for instance in many recipes for funchi. It can be milled into flour, cooked whole as porridge, or even brewed into beer.

The Krobo people of Ghana mark the yam harvest with the weeklong Ngmayem thanksgiving festival. Millet is one of the staple crops of the Sukuma of Tanzania; in addition to the bugobogobo dance that inspires this piece, the Sukuma have a tradition of milletthreshing songs called itula.

Let Us Dance

A time to make merry,
Feet impatient to dance:
See the children run about,
Jump around and prance.

There will be
Sweet potatoes,
So come, fellow farmer,
Let us dance Bugobogobo.

Wish for abundance
As harvest comes round.
Seeds that were sown:
Now the millet that abounds.

There will be
Cash crop tobacco.
So come, fellow farmer,
Let us dance Bugobogobo.

I'm of the Sukuma,
A part of the Bantu.
Observance of nature,
Then we take the cue.

There will be
The trusty hoe,
So come, fellow farmer,
Let us dance Bugobogobo.

Bugobogobo is a celebratory dance associated with agricultural labor, from the Sukuma people of Tanzania. Song of staple and adult relaxation; verses of ancestral libation.

NATAL CYCAD

umguza, isigqiki-somkhovi, *Encephalartos natalensis*

Cycads resemble stout palm trees or giant ferns, but they are more closely related to pine trees, and like them they bear cones— several feet long, in some cases. Pollen from male plants' cones is brought to the female plants' seed-bearing cones by long-nosed weevils: these plants existed long before traditional pollinators like bees and butterflies. While today monkeys disperse the seeds, once cycad cones were eaten and excreted by the brontosaurus. The plant's stem has been used worldwide as a source of sago, a traditional starchy foodstuff, but contains a neurotoxin that must be carefully washed away.

Cycads establish a symbiotic relationship with nitrogen-fixing cyanobacteria in the soil and share the nitrogen and carbon with other nearby organisms. The trees are also some of the world's most endangered species. In the great Modjadji Cycad Reserve mentioned in the PREFACE grow trees protected by the Rain Queen of the BaLobedu Baga Modjadji.

One name for the Natal cycad is *isigqiki-somkhovu*, zombie's chair or pillow, presumably because if a zombie approaches a homestead surrounded by cycads, it will rest atop the cycad and the home will remain safe. Many African cycads are located in areas with frequent lightning strikes— indeed, fire is a stimulus for the trees to produce cones. This chant describes the Mpondo people's use of Natal cycad (Xhosa: *umguza*) to ward off magic and lightning as part of a protective practice called ukubethelela.

Umguza

Over in South Africa,
Umguza.
Into Pondoland,
Umguza.
Planted round the home,
Umguza.
Counteracting sorcery,
Umguza.
Bulwark against lightning,
Umguza.
Ukubethelela,
Umguza.

NUTMEG

Myristica fragrans, miski, noz-moscada, muskaatboom

"A lovely lady in a boat, wearing a red petticoat": that's how Grenadians riddlingly refer to the spice their island now produces in great quantity. The large seed that is nutmeg is enclosed in a lattice of bright red mace (the "petticoat"), all resting in a fleshy outer shell (the "boat") that is similar in color and shape to an apricot.

Grenada is a relative newcomer to nutmeg production. Once, the Banda Islands (now part of Indonesia) were the world's only source of nutmeg, which made the spice incredibly valuable. The Dutch, keen to control the spice trade at its source, took control of the islands and then committed genocide against the Bandanese, resettling the islands with coerced laborers from elsewhere in their empire.

The Dutch monopoly lasted until the nineteenth century, when the British took control of the Banda Islands and sent *M. fragrans* specimens throughout their empire for transplanting. Nutmeg trees took root in Southern India and in parts of the Caribbean, particularly Grenada.

West Africa has its own nutmeg tree, the beautiful *Monodora myristica*, a SOURSOP relative whose seed is sometimes called "calabash nutmeg." So when nutmeg reached the Caribbean, the spice naturally became a part of diasporic cuisine, including jerk seasoning. Either type of nutmeg may be used today in West African jollof. Nutmeg also serves many healing purposes, including oral hygiene, helping the digestion, and soothing neuralgia, often in conjunction with salvia (sage) or other herbs. (see GERANIUM.)

The Nutmeg Princess

From Indonesia to Grenada,
Journey of *Myristica*,
Across the oceans and seas.
Inhale one, twice, thrice,
You're on the island called Spice.

(*chanted*)
Beautiful, beautiful,
Enchantingly beautiful,
With diamonds in her hair.

The others wanted the jewels
That adorned her plaited hair.
All Aglo and Petal wanted
Was to be in the presence
Of the Nutmeg Princess.

(*chanted*)
Beautiful, beautiful,
Enchantingly beautiful,
With diamonds in her hair.

She advises the two youth
To care for all

And to believe in themselves.
They became the caretakers
Of the fruit and nutmeg trees.

(*chanted*)
Beautiful, beautiful,
Enchantingly beautiful,
With diamonds in her hair.

A touch of the Solomonic in a tale contrasting the desire for wealth of most of the villagers and the desire for knowledge of two of the younger residents. In the end, no one gets a diamond, but the two youth receive the guardianship of the nutmeg trees, transforming the island into a "nutmeg paradise." During his Grenadian childhood, I imagine that Theo Marryshow, the future "Father of the West Indian Federation," would have been the first around the fire, waiting to hear of Anancy, soucouyants, or any of the other characters that spangled his formative evenings.

OKRA

ilà, quiabo, quimbombó,
Abelmoschus esculentus

The ridged, velvety pods of okra, perhaps the best known vegetable of the African diaspora, are familiar enough that most people have an opinion on the plant's mucilaginous qualities. But fewer have seen the okra plant itself: a close relative of HIBISCUS (and until recently assigned to the same genus) which quickly reaches the size and width of a shrub, with ephemeral, crepe-like blossoms and cranberry-red stems the color of roselle. Its pods enjoy great popularity in West and Southern Africa, as well as in India and the Philippines, but its leaves, which share the pods' slimy texture, are edible as well. Within decades of the first slave ships' arrival, enslaved Africans had brought okra (or [ki]ngombo—the Kimbundu term for the plant, origin of the term gumbo) to Brazil and were teaching Indigenous people to grow and prepare it; it soon became part of Europeans' diet there as well. Okra was commonplace in the provision grounds of enslaved people and in maroon communities throughout the New World. Among followers of Candomblé and Umbanda, the plant is sacred, but it is avoided by practitioners of the Kongo-derived Cuban religion Palo Mayombe.

In Yoruban diasporic religions, amalá de Xangô (a.k.a. amalá ila or amalá con quimbombó) is the ritual dish offered to the orisha Shango. It is a stew made of chopped okra, onion, dried shrimp, and palm oil. Amalá is served on Wednesdays at the pegi, or altar, on a large tray decorated with twelve upright, uncooked okra. Dried okra soaked with leaves of a MALLOW species may be used to wash Shango's tools.

The Okra Man

Did you ever come across the Okra Man?
Eats his favorite green
Whenever he can.
His other name is Shango:
Deity of the element that warms the food.

Okra with porridge:
He likes his cornmeal.
Okra with shrimps,
Alongside palm oil.
Okra with beef
And a touch of yam.

So have you encountered the Okra Man?
Relishing ila
From the offering pan.
His other name is Shango:
Deity of the force that generates the forge.

Shango is said to be a historic figure, an alaafin (king) of Oyo—hence the title "Okra Man"—who was deified posthumously as an orisha.

155

ONION

Allium spp., cebolla, xonacatl

The alliums comprise a large genus notable for the pungent aroma and a root bulb with high sulfur content, which helps protect it from pests. Its most well-known members—onion, garlic, shallot, leek—are originally temperate Eurasian species. A few are native to Africa, although the perennial "Egyptian" walking onion actually originated on the Indian subcontinent, perhaps coming to Europe with the Roma people.

Columbus, arriving in Hispaniola in 1494, found no onions there and instructed his crew to plant some. But in fact many allium species are native to the New World. The name "Chicago" comes from the Irenwa word for a type of wild onion. The 16th-century Florentine Codex contains a few Nahuatl riddles about Mexico's pre-conquest allium—"What is a small white stone holding a quetzal feather? The onion!"—which give us some idea about the plant's appearance: a little bulb with emerald leaves, the color of the quetzal's plumage.

Onion belongs to no particular orisha, though a dish cooked with onion is appreciated by Oya. In Puerto Rican folklore, a cebollita or Little Onion teams up with Little Vine and Juan Bobo to become the main antagonist in the Battle of the Tiger, retold here.

Tale of Little Onion

When Jah Folk asked us to think of magnificent duos, someone said, "Nelson Mandela and Walter Sisulu," which met with approval, exclamations, and touching of fists; the same with the mention of Martin Luther King and Ralph Abernathy. Our local hero suggested Léopold Senghor and Birago Diop and also Aimé Césaire and Léon Damas, reminding us of thinkers and writers from the Francophone world.

Then he told us of Juan Bobo and Little Onion: Juan Bobo, the lovable buffoon of Hispanic Caribbean folklore, and his onetime ally, Little Onion from the Allium crew. They came together in the fight against Tiger, who'd killed the pet donkey of Juan. A tale from Puerto Rico, which Jah Folk said he'd first read in a collection compiled by one of his heroines, Pura Belpré, legendary storyteller of the New York library system, who told stories in Spanish and English.

Yes, Little Onion,
Come, Little Onion,
You and I counteracting tiger.

Jump into the pot,

Your place of hiding,
Ingredients bubbling away.

Sing, Little Onion,
Don't stop, Little Onion,
Raising his pressure level.

Bounce out of the pot,
Into his eyes,
Utilizing your burning skills.

Bless you, Little Onion,
Always, Little Onion!
We defeated our nemesis.

ORANGE

Citrus × *sinensis*, syn. *Citrus* × *aurantium*
f. *aurantium*, orange douce, laranjeira,
naranjo

Oranges grow on shortish trees with waxy, pointed leaves, and what the fruit looks like is known to just about everyone. The fruit that most people eat is a sweet orange, which emerged as a result of selective breeding somewhere in Europe around 1450—by contrast with the bitter or Seville orange, which has a history that starts in China and was brought to Spain by Islamic cultivators in the 10th century. Individual orange trees are in their own way a synthetic product too, since almost all of them are grafted combinations of a hardy root stock with branch stock selected to give flavorful fruit.

Sweet orange trees were one of the plants that Columbus brought with him to the Caribbean. They grow well on Caribbean islands like Jamaica and Trinidad, where street vendors sell them when they're in season. The fruit is delicious, of course— one Caribbean preparation is to serve it with a little bit of salt— but the leaves and flowers also have culinary and medicinal uses. Oranges may be given to Oshun, the orisha of love.

Orange Tree Fly Whisk

When it comes to counteracting heat and shooing away insects, I've heard of the use of a fan, record sleeve, newspaper, book, hand, magazine, or whisk, but never of an orange tree—until I got comfortable on my sofa, under the quilt, took a little time out, and went to Haiti.

You see, African and Caribbean folklore has produced a few characters who like to uproot trees, either for personal use or to help a beloved mother. In the Haitian case, it's the former. But Sunjata, hero of the Mandinka, had a more complicated reason for displacing one of the Monumental Ones.

Sunjata was born without the use of his legs to a hunchbacked mother—you can imagine the level of bullying and ostracism they faced. Yearly, during the time of manhood initiation, mothers cook a meal for their sons, who gather the baobab leaves for them. Not being able to climb, Sunjata can't get the required items, and the wound goes deeper. Since the wound he carries is now unbearable, he commissions the blacksmith to forge him an iron bar. With this implement, he raises himself, and for the first time in his life, he stands erect. And what do you think is the first thing he does? He goes straight to the village baobab tree, dislodges it completely, and replants it in his mother's compound. So all the women and their sons who have hounded them over the years, like Paul before conversion, will now have to come within their former victims' gates to get the necessary ingredient.

Now, in the tale from Haiti, Break Mountain is a gargantuan youth, so huge that he disturbs ecosystems and communities with each step he takes. One day the mosquitos are bugging him. Why they would want to be around him is anybody's guess! Maybe they were running him ragged because of past disruptions, trying to bring about at least a semblance of revenge. It's a hot day; the forest is steaming. Each piece of sweat that falls from him becomes a raging river, and each movement of his agitated arm generates a windstorm. Finally, at the finale of patience, he uproots an orange tree. Then, with one swoop of it, he sends the little irritants to God knows where. And Break Mountain goes on his way, giving thanks for *Citrus sinensis*.

As well as giving us the book that inspired this piece, I think Harold Courlander gave us the greatest anthology of African oral traditions when he presented us with A Treasury of African Folklore.

In the piece above, orange is a momentary feature, but there are two others from Haiti in which this fruit has the leading role. In one story, "The One Who Would Not Listen to His Own Dream," a young traveler sleeps under an orange tree, receives a dream about a citrus remedy, and heals a princess. In the other from Haiti, "The Magic Orange Tree," a hungry girl defeats her wicked stepmother with the help of the eponymous tree. In one from Brazil, "Tasi and the Oranges," a young howler monkey learns a lesson the hard way.

161

PALM

Elaeis guineensis, palma africana, oil palm, epo

The African Oil Palm is a palm tree that grows about sixty feet tall and develops clusters of dark red fruits that contain a very high proportion of oil. It originated in tropical West Africa, where people used and still use it in cooking, medicine, and religion. So great were the profits in trading this product of silviculture that European merchants named the coast of Nigeria the Gulf of Palm Oil.

European colonizers spread palm oil trees all over the world. In the tropics of Asia and the Americas, it grows in massive monocropped plantations, often on land stolen by corporate growers from farmers and Indigenous peoples. In Africa, where it still has to contend with the old pests and diseases, the oil palm mostly grows in ecological balance with its environment and provides those who harvest it with a nutritious, long-lasting cooking oil.

In Yoruba religion, the kernels of the palm fruit are used for the immensely complex form of divination known as Ifa, which is based in a sixteen-principle system involving a literary corpus of sixteen books, the odu, each sixteen chapters long. Awos or priests hence cast 16 consecrated palm nuts, *ikin,* to consult the oracle. Such a consultation is the topic of this piece.

Babalawo Chant

Tell me,
Arecacea,
Will I attract her?
Tell me, Babalawo.

Tell me,
Arecacea,
Time for Ifa,
Tell me, Babalawo:
Throw the palm nuts for me.

Tell me,
Arecacea,
Through the diviner,
Tell me, Babalawo.

Tell me,
Arecacea,
Her and I together
Tell me, Babalawo:
Throw the palm nuts for me.

PAPAYA

ibepe, pawpaw, mamão, fruta bomba, *Carica papaya*

Papaya, like BANANA, is strictly speaking an herb rather than a tree, although it can grow up to thirty feet tall. Its stem is hollow and green, not a woody trunk, and the plant lives only five to ten years. Papaya leaves are big and palmate, somewhat like fig leaves, and the papaya fruits grow directly on the trunklike stem. Wild papayas are dioecious, with the fruit-bearing plants being female, the pollen-bearing ones male, but thousands of years ago Mesoamerican peoples began to domesticate the plants and played a role in selecting for a third sex, perfect or hermaphrodite, to which most cultivated papayas belong.

The Spanish colonist Gonzalo Fernández de Oviedo became, in 1526, the first European to record an encounter with papaya; he was somewhere in the Antilles, where it had been brought from the mainland by the Taíno people, who grew it in their gardens. Soon the papaya reached Asia, and its Arawakan name, ababaia, transformed as it traveled, to papya, pempe and pawpaw. (In North America, "pawpaw" also designates an unrelated fruit tree, a cousin of SOURSOP.)

In Yoruba medicine, root, fruit, and leaf can be used medicinally, accompanied by incantations extolling the plant, such as "Papaya never fails to cure diseases." In Candomblé practice, a syrup is made from the male flowers and used to help with chest cold. From the fruit's latex, the enzyme papain is extracted. Meso- and South Americans have long used the papain-rich unripe fruit to tenderize meat, and papain is now sold in commercial tenderizers.

Lady Papaya

Lady Papaya,
You and a prayer:
Presentation to deity.

Man of Bahia
With a gift for orisha,
Kneeling there at the shrine.

Temple of Oya,
Song of Yoruba,
Verses of Fon and Bantu.

Lady Papaya,
Sacred provider,
Paying homage to Yemoja.

For Leo Paninho, Denise Pantera, Ronke Fadare, Fiona Spence-Reid, and Emilie Belibi Because the fruit is amongst the offerings that can be brought to the female orishas Yemoja (motherhood and the sea) and Oya (wind and storms) at their respective temples, this piece is entitled "Lady Papaya."

The beliefs of the Fon (Benin), Ewe (Togo and Ghana), and Bantu (originally from the southern borderland region of Nigeria/Cameroon and resident in central, eastern, and southern Africa), also influenced the spirituality of enslaved people in the Americas and their descendants, alongside that of the Yoruba of Nigeria. The houses of Candomblé in Brazil are good examples of the blending of these traditions.

PEA

cowpea, black-
eyed pea, *Vigna
unguiculata*

The Anansi story told in this piece exists in many variations with many different crops, but the cowpea or black-eyed pea is important wherever Anansi has traveled. Once, this garden pea relative grew wild among rocks and acacias in the Sahel, the savanna that stretches from Mali to Sudan. Around 6000 years ago, people in various parts of Africa began to domesticate the resilient plant, along with MILLET and SORGHUM, with which it is often intercropped. In the time of the pharaohs, the pea traveled throughout Africa, to Europe, and beyond, reaching Southeast Asia by 400 BCE, where it was bred into the yardlong or asparagus bean—better suited than a dry bean to the humidity of its new home.

Black-eyed peas came to the Americas on the Middle Passage and were grown by enslaved Africans in provision grounds. In Africa, the peas were and are often a festive food, to be ground and fried in rich palm oil (dendê) on celebratory occasions. Echoes of this tradition remains today in the US South, where the peas stand for good luck at New Year's and are often served as part of Hoppin' John, a dish made of black-eyed peas and rice with smoked pork. In Brazil, the West African fritters, akara, became acarajé, still fried in dendê, and are sold on the streets by Bahian women clad in white cutwork dresses and head-scarves. The dish is grounded in Candomblé ritual; it is an offering, first to Exu (Eshu) and then to Oya, Shango, and other orishas.

Tale of a Pea Harvest

I wish the whole of Kingston could have fitted into Papine Square on that night that became a comedy night, live and direct, right there in our beloved place. And the theme carrying humor was Anansi, generating one of the legendary evenings in Papine Square.

It began with a story told by Jah Folk about the arachnid supremo and yams. Following this, one of the vendors told one about himself; then, like a relay team, others took the baton and told a tale of Eight Legs, offering the funniest they knew. Another vendor gave us one. Shanty Man, passing by, shared another. So did a neighbor of Tommy's and mine, a UWI student, a local pastor, and so on. And each tale topped up the laughter pool like a sparkling stream feeding the spangled river.

As he was delivering a workshop at Papine High the following morning, Jah Folk told the final one to conclude the evening: another tale from Greed Gorge, where the protagonist always endeavors to indulge himself—at the gorging time—in his secret ravine. He told a tale of a pea harvest and the decision to die! Yes, Anansi pretends to pass away! An elaborate ruse, involving a funeral! Before he "expires," he asks for a hole to be cut in the coffin and a pot of water placed on the grave. Although frustrated, Aso, his long-suffering wife, goes along with it; she believes him when he says it's a way to guard the harvest from animals and humans. But as you've guessed, he sneaks out every night, boiling and enjoying a supper of peas.

Aso and the family are perplexed at the case of the disappearing peas—all except the eldest son, who has become wise to his father's shenanigans. He makes a figure using a stump of tree, branches, tar and a hat. That moonless night, Anansi emerges from his place of ploy. Thinking it's a friend come to visit him, he embraces the effigy...and is stuck! Next morning, running from public shame and damnation, he hides in the roofbeams, where he tends to reside to this day.

Jah Folk wondered whether her family and community held a vigil for poor Aso—each one lighting a candle and saying a prayer for the committed wife who's tearing out her last hair.

Brings me to my knees,
With his escapade of peas.
Generates high fever,
I splutter and wheeze.
I beg you, Creator,
Watch over that husband of mine.
Watch over Anansi,
I beg you, please.

One hustle after another,
Quick as a sneeze.
He is lava running,

I pray for cool breeze.
I beg you, Creator,
Watch over that husband of mine.
Watch over Anansi,
I beg you, please.

To all of us, blessed to have gathered there, it seemed like God had said, "Let laughter be the dominant activity in Papine Square this evening." And so it was.

For my son, Bingy Samuels, because peas are his favorite vegetable.

PEANUT

Arachis hypogea, amendoim, maní, cacahuete

Peanuts are the edible seeds of a short, leafy plant in the legume family. When it gets to be about a foot tall, long pointed pegs called peduncles grow from the plant's faded flowers into the ground. It is these pegs that grow peanuts, not the plant's roots.

The peanut was first domesticated in the area of present-day Argentina or Brazil, but became popular in Africa after Portuguese introduced it there as a staple crop for slave ships in the 16th century, perhaps due in part to its similarity to the (less productive) Bambara groundnut. When enslaved Africans found peanuts growing in the Caribbean, they were already familiar with the crop, and peanuts were an important food for Maroon settlements. The peanut probably spread to the United States from Africa: "goober," a US slang term for peanut, comes from the Kongo language via the Afro-English creole Gullah. In the US South, peanuts were once used to woo ladies, and were served at outdoor dances. Roasted peanuts are a frequent offering in Vodou ceremonies, particularly to the loas called Guede or Gede.

Tale of Peanuts

Can't recall right now whether Jah Folk had taken us to Suriname before, but he did that evening in Papine Square: took us to the land where they speak Sranan Tongo. He told us of our friends *Arachis*, who have given us so much: the morning porridge, so we can commence the day with positivity; the punch of afternoon refreshment; the sauce accompanying the rice of evening enjoyment. So peanuts, like humans, deserve the truth.

If the farmer says he's going to harvest on a certain day, so it should be. Only the imprisoned want to leave before their time. Here comes Farmer, wanting to deface the sacred oath between Soil and Man. There is a time to harvest and that is that: ancient fact. Here comes Farmer, breaking his pact with peanuts.

So they protest, rebel.

And his walking stick protests also, in solidarity with peanuts.

And so does the stool, standing beside the *Arachis* fighters.

Household items of quiet residence rise up, carrying the peanut pennant. I imagine them: peanuts, hoe, stool, adze, pestle, and other rebels, jiggling, bouncing around, jeering at the one intending to break the longtime pact. Faced with such an onslaught of vocal rebellion from soil and from hearth, the farmer relents, re-signing the Protocols of Sacred Oath. Throughout Suriname, the residents of soil and their guardians sing a song of peanut power.

Tommy and I walked home, hoping our respective parents would make peanut porridge for breakfast.

There is a variation of this tale from Nevis called "Things That Talked." Peanuts (or groundnuts) feature in a story from the Central African Republic, "The Leopard, The Dog and the Squirrel," about false accusation and capital punishment. In one from the Lunda of Zambia, Kalulu the Hare defeats his in-laws, who are cheating him of his peanut crop, with the help of his friend Bushbuck.

PEAR

pera, poire, *Pyrus* spp.,
kummatrà

The pear, coming in varieties with names like Bartlett, Hirschbirne, and d'Anjou, might seem the quintessental Northern European fruit, and *Pyrus communis* does prefer a cool, temperate climate. But the *Pyrus* genus originated in China, not Europe, and Asia is where *P. pyrifolia*, the round "Asian pear" sold in supermarkets today, was domesticated. From there it spread to Asia Minor and the Caucasus, where the fruit we now call "pyriform" (but which some early authors referred to as "calabash-shaped"!) first emerged. The Chechens of the North Caucasus once held pear trees to be sacred, the abode of good spirits; to fell a pear tree was forbidden.

In the orchards of al-Andalus (Muslim Spain), pears were among the most highly prized and widely cultivated fruit trees. The master farmers there nurtured countless varieties through seed propaga-tion and grafting, growing them as part of a biodiverse agroeco-system along with bananas, date palms, and watermelon. A great diversity of pears can still be found in Spain; not by coincidence does this tale of Tía Miseria's pear tree have Iberian roots.

Pears became a dooryard staple in southern gardens, too, especially after 19th-century pomologists began to trial the more heat-tolerant Asian species. Pear preserves sat next to guava jelly in the pantry of the young Zora Neale Hurston's Florida home; a pear tree a key character in *Their Eyes Were Watching God*. The Monterrey pear or "home pear," popular in kitchen gardens, was developed in Mexico and came north to Texas. Not a commercial crop, but backyard bounty: perhaps the story of Old Aunt Misery will play itself out again.

Pear Tree Blues

Reflecting on one of the stories from Puerto Rico reminded me again of my boyhood days, especially during the summer break. Wandering the country lanes outside the town, we were opportunistic little robbers, raiding the village gardens for a booty called apples. For the boys in the story our folklorist told, the objective was pears. Whereas we attempted to take from any tree that offered reward, these two targeted just one particular tree—unwittingly opening the sluice gates to suffering.

So in this story, there's an old woman known as Ol' Aunt Misery who was granted a wish by a penitent on his way to God. The wish she makes is one of adhesion, a prayer for glue. She desired that one surface should stick to another—in this case, flesh to bark.

> We brought it on ourselves,
> Better watch out for misery.
> Brought it on ourselves,
> Better watch out for misery.
> Began with an old woman
> And an old pear tree.

After an extended time kissing bark and urinating down the trunk, the boys were released from their time of tree adhesiveness, vowing never to take again from their tree of yearning and prize.

Now, seeing the success of her ploy, when Death comes visiting, Ol' Aunt Misery makes one last request: that he pick a pear or two for her last enjoyment. So you can imagine what happens. Yes—the one who reaps gets stuck to the tree!

And while the grim one is unavailable, no one dies. So certain people suffer. The local carpenter lost more than a few commissions because no one needed a coffin. The undertaker was seriously considering taking up another profession after thirty years of facilitating rest. So these and other professionals, such as the medical ones, affected by the loss of their death-based income, began to relentlessly petition and berate Death. Fed up with the vocal onslaught and enforced stay, he makes a pact with the old woman: release from the pear tree for him, immortality for her.

And that's how misery began to meander its way around the world again.

> We brought it on ourselves,
> Better watch out for misery.
> Brought it on ourselves,
> Better watch out for misery.
> Began with an old woman
> And an old pear tree.

PINE

Pinus caribaea var. *bahamensis*, yellow pine, pino amarillo

The Caribbean pine is endemic to the Bahamas, its only native pine tree and the dominant species in the "pineyard" ecosystems unique to the northern islands of the Lucayan archipelago (the Bahamas and Turks and Caicos.) The tree takes root in pockets of soil amid the porous limestone that forms the islands—and the underwater pits offshore, the "blue holes" mentioned in this piece.

The pines became common when humans, the Lucayan Taíno, arrived on the islands in around 800 BCE and began farming. They used a slash-and-burn technique to clear space for *conucos*, mounds of crops that included TOBACCO, cotton, and CASSAVA. Unlike hardwoods, the pines are fire-resistant, and they require abundant light to germinate and thrive;

low-intensity fires benefit them by clearing away underbrush. Now pines support species from boas to bats and rare birds. The pineyards of one island in the archipelago, Abaco, are home to the colorful Bahama parrot, who nests in cavities in the forest floor.

European colonizers used the pines' timber for ship masts and their pitch to make the vessels watertight. Beginning in the early 20th century, companies came to log the pines intensively, clear-cutting the old-growth trees; when these were gone, pulpwood companies moved in for the new growth. Today, the pines have been left to regrow, but an introduced scale insect threatens the population on some of the islands. For many reasons, the pines need a guardian.

Pine Tree Guardian

I saw a man today, sitting under a *Pinus caribea*. I've seen him sitting under the same tree before. While the yellowthroat sat and sang and Racoon continued his unknown mission, the seated man reminded me of Silamaka, the Fulani hero, who favored a tamarind tree before and after battle: for composure before and for reflection after.

You know how it is when you're people-watching: your mind sometimes wanders, creating vignettes, writing biographies in brief, around the people you're observing. Because I'd seen him there before, I began to think of him as the guardian of the pine trees, the solitary sentinel, like Fetefete, who performs protective duties for the safu tree, or Iroko, orisha of the eponymous tree sacred to the Yoruba. I wondered about his night shift duties—whether he used a lamp, torch or candles.

Because of his guardianship of non-human life, maybe he's the only one Lusca allows to swim in peace. Lusca, the scourge of the waters around Andros Island, said to be a fusion of octopus and shark. Lusca, feared by fishermen, sailors, and parents. To stop the more adventurous children from swimming near the blue holes—the deepest, most cavernous parts of the waters—the adults would remind their charges of the monstrous hybrid who resides there, enjoying his hobby of capsizing boats and snatching people. Yes, it could be that the one sitting there is the only human who can swim near the blue holes—always floating a portion of pinecones to Lusca before stepping into the water.

Anyway, he picked a perfect spot: green behind and turquoise in front, pink orchids one side of him, snow-berries the other side, looking out over the Atlantic. For a moment, I envied the Pine Tree Guardian as I rushed past him, seeing him sitting there amid aroma, blessed by panorama, cocooned in peace on Andros Island in the Bahamas.

PINEAPPLE

Ananas comosus, piña, ananas, abacaxi

The pineapple is a spiky, oblong compound fruit that develops out of the dramatically crimson compound flower of a shrub that belongs to the bromeliad family. One of the first Europeans to see one in the New World said that the pineapple looked like an artichoke; you may or may not be able to see the resemblance.

Though people associate pineapples with Hawaii, they were first domesticated somewhere in Central America and served as a staple crop throughout the region.

When the Spanish took them back to Europe, pineapple mania swept the continent and enormous pineapple plantations were established throughout the colonized world—eventually, in Hawaii too.

Pineapples are still grown in much of the Caribbean, usually as part of a mixed small farm rather than on plantations. The plants are easy to propagate: next time you buy one from the store, you can chop off the top and plant it and grow a pineapple shrub of your own.

Little Pineapple Child

Don't fret, little one,
Dry your waterfall eyes.
There will be other days
For hopscotch and tag.

Let's go down by the river
To speak with ol' man Heron,
After he's sung the Saga of Differences.
Verse of *Ananas comosus*,
Stanza of *Homo sapiens*,
Chorus of everyone.

Come on,
Hop on my back,
Piggyback though Paradise Park,
And after peanut butter sandwiches,
Race you all the way
Up towards Heaven Heath.

And next time you play hide and seek,
I may play also.
So don't let their teasing disturb you,
Verbal torment send you wild.
We'll touch our fists together,
Little Pineapple Child.

PLANTAIN

Musa × ssp., borode, platano, banana-da-terra

Plantain and BANANA are, botanically speaking, not so much trees as they are giant herbs. The term "plantain" can refer to any *Musa* used for cooking, but "true" plantains are triploid cultivars of the AAB type, most of which were domesticated in Central and West Africa after ancestral plantains arrived from Asia, probably via Madagascar, 2000-3000 years ago. Like bananas, they became a staple crop; they re milled into flour and also feature in fufu, along with yams and cassava. Dried plantain skins are also a possible ingredient in black soap, as described in this piece.

Plantains became prolific in the provision grounds of enslaved people, along with YAM and TARO, crops with similar cultivation histories. These starchy foodstuffs would join CASSAVA and BREAD-FRUIT to form the classic *vianda* portion of the Caribbean meal. Plantains star in diasporic fufu descendants such as mofongo and mangú, and in the Spanish-speaking Caribbean, it is said that a foreigner who has fully adopted the local culture is *aplatanado/a*—"plantainized."

Song of Plantain and Cocoa

PLANTAIN: Once I hung, now I'm a pile. Yes, once I was fruit, now I am ash. But I live on: I am Plantain.

COCOA: Like Plantain beside me, they use my covering; like Brother P, I am reduced to ash: I am Cocoa.

PLANTAIN AND COCOA: We are ash, we are ash, content of potash, in the making of Dudu Osun.

PLANTAIN: Be good to interact again, Sister Sweet, with Camwood and Honey.

COCOA: Palm Oil and Shea.

PLANTAIN: Lime Juice and Water.

COCOA: And Aloe Vera.

PLANTAIN: Yes, as we all become soap.

COCOA: The crucial black soap of their living.

PLANTAIN: Necessary abstergent.

COCOA: Yes, old friend. And as well as the aforementioned, we know we shall encounter Iyerosun.

PLANTAIN: Yes, the sacred dust.

COCOA: Of termite production.

PLANTAIN: From the camwood tree.

COCOA: Known also as African sandalwood.

PLANTAIN: What would they do without us?

COCOA: Suffer.

PLANTAIN: What do they do with us?

COCOA: Triumph.

PLANTAIN: With leaf or fruit.

COCOA: Bark or root.

PLANTAIN: African Breadfruit, overpowering limitations.

COCOA: Elephant Grass, to reduce domination.

PLANTAIN: Melon, counteracting infertility.

COCOA: Balsam Apple, to generate stability.

PLANTAIN AND COCOA: We are ash, we are ash, content of potash, in the making of Dudu Osun.

COCOA: As well as the sacred powder, the sacred text.

PLANTAIN: Yes, Sister Sweet, the Odu Ifa, pathway to wisdom.

COCOA: Babalawo invocation.

PLANTAIN: I've heard the words of the iyalawo, priestess of Ifa.

COCOA: I've heard the words of the babalawo, priest of Ifa.

PLANTAIN: Given to them through Orunmila,

COCOA: Their orisha of divination, disseminating knowledge.

PLANTAIN: We are all part of their spiritual sustenance; Odu Ifa, Iyerosun, Dudu Osun, all empowered by Ewe.

COCOA: Of course Brother P! Ewe: you and I and all the other plants.

PLANTAIN: Yes, Sister Sweet. Water Cabbage dispels the negative.

COCOA: Banana simplifies how we live.

PLANTAIN: Sugarcane, to sweeten character.

COCOA: Sweet Potato, supporting the survivor.

PLANTAIN: We work alongside all of them for the upliftment of humanity.

PLANTAIN AND COCOA: We are ash, we are ash, content of potash, in the making of Dudu Osun.

As well as God, known as Olorun, the Yoruba have four hundred and one orishas (deities). Orunmila is the orisha of wisdom and the form of divination called Ifa. He has a close connection to Osanyin, orisha of plants and healing.

Odu Ifa (sacred text) and Iyerosun (sacred dust) are part of Ifa divination; Dudu Osun, the black soap of West Africa, is used spiritually, as in Orisha belief, as well as medicinally.

PUMPKIN

ithanga, *Cucurbita* spp., joumou,
manhanga, ijodo, abóbora

"Yes! Pumpkins!" wrote Frederick Douglass in his newspaper *The North Star.* "We raised a nice lot of them this season in our own garden. Some of them were very large—yellow as the gold of California—and as deliciously sweet as ever pleased the taste of the most fastidious epicure, or appeased the appetite of the most hungry laborer. It does us good to look upon those pumpkins.... The ground was prepared—seed sown—and the plant cultivated by our own colored hands." For Douglass and for other abolitionists, the pumpkin patch stood as the antithesis of the plantation, producing low-maintenance, non-cash crops. This symbolism meant that Thanksgiving pumpkin pie was long rejected by white Southerners—in favor, ironically, of sweet potato pie, a culinary tradition of the formerly enslaved.

The *Cucurbita* genus was domesticated in Mesoamerica ten thousand years ago, the earliest of any known crop, and its members have long been integral to the foodways of Indigenous Americans from Canada to Cuba. The turban squash or *joumou* (from Tupi *jirumum*: *C. maxima*) is the eponymous ingredient in Haiti's renowned independence soup. If grilled, this squash may be part of an offering to Papa Legba.

In parts of Africa, pumpkins (*C. maxima/moschata*) are consumed three to four times a week during the rainy season, especially the leaves, but also the fruit, in a dish with corn called isijingi. Both pumpkin and corn are planted in the Nomdede festival, where Zulu maidens pay homage to the fertility goddess Nomkhubulwane.

The Pumpkin Chant

I've never known a man,
Nomkhubulwane.
To take part in Nomdede,
Nomkhubulwane.
Only women take part,
Nomkhubulwane.
In a special garden,
Nomkhubulwane.
On a hillside in Spring,
Nomkhubulwane.
A libation is made,
Nomkhubulwane.
We plant pumpkin seeds,
Nomkhubulwane.
Plus sorghum and corn,
Nomkhubulwane.
We dance and we sing,
Nomkhubulwane.
She's rainbow and mist,
Nomkhubulwane.
Rain and the harvest,
Nomkhubulwane.

RASPBERRY

Rubus idaeus, 'ullayq, frambuesa

Raspberries and their kin—black-berries, dewberries, salmonber-ries, cloudberries, and nearly 700 others—belong to the rose family and share the rose's thorns. They're brambles by another name—but this doesn't have to be a bad thing. In a well-known folktale (one that melds African and Cherokee tradition) Br'er Rabbit uses his affinity for the briar-patch to outwit his enemies. Indeed, by keeping out predators, dense bramble thickets become ecosystems unto themselves for smaller creatures. Birds nest there, moths feed there, and the flowers attract countless pollinators.

Raspberries are relative newcomers to the world of human cultivation. Although humans have enjoyed the bounty of their local *Rubus* species since prehistoric times, we seem to have begun trying to breed them for certain qualities only within the past 500 years. The notorious wineberry and Himalayan black-berry, deemed weeds in North America, were both brought to the continent as grafting stock to improve the native varieties. Members of the species hybridize with ease, but the thorns and two-year fruiting cycle still pose an obstacle to making the berries profitable. In many respects, *Rubus* remains an unruly, untamed genus, and whether we forage or grow them, berries are quintessentially a gift, as this piece reminds us.

Redemption Raspberries

I beg you, Elegua,
You, the signposter,
Please show me the way to go.
A portion of raspberries,
The type "Ruby Beauty":
I bring you the *Rubus* glow.

*I think I need to go back to the crossroads and decide
again. I know the shadow is always; it's not going anywhere; I created it and it remains. But I would like to
uproot myself from where I'm embedded. Lay the stepping stones, orisha of roads, and I will follow.*

I found a spot where the sun comes in. You know how she
is; she gets kind of restless like some of us, here one minute,
gone the next; but I found a place she likes to stay when
she steps into my garden. It is the *Rubus* corner.

Once I'd chosen the spot, which has some shelter, the
mission of removal began: taking out the unwanted. The
clearing away and the weeding, to give the future offerings the best beginning possible, enhanced by what the
horse expels.

Some offer guava,
Others chili pepper;
I am the bringer of raspberries.

I was never one for raspberries, not really a berry man, apart from the occasional strawberry, but if genus *Rubus* is part of the redemption package, I'll plant the little red ones as far as the eye can see.

But tell me, how many get ensnared at the crossroads, mired in indecision? Was hope mislaid between Limbo Lane and Avenue Apathy? Is it easier, safer to linger at the crossroads than to choose a road?

And then putting in the posts and bamboo canes; after all, we all need a little support here and there, for whatever reason; and maybe protection too. Who will put a net around the smallest, youngest one, during his first time in detention? I place one over the gifts to you.

Some offer ginger,
Others angelica;
I am the bringer of raspberries.

You have opened the gates, so there is a choice of pathways. Is this choice rooted in personal history? Group experience? Family pressure? Religious conviction? Political zeal? One of these, or a mixture of them? Deity of directions, guide us on.

The soil is well drained and I go easy with the watering; no gardener wants to commit the sin of waterlogging. And I have grown them for summer fruiting and for autumn-time too; I've grown "All Gold" and I've grown "Autumn Bliss," and mulch has made a contribution to the growth.

> Some offer heather,
> Others gardenia;
> I am the bringer of raspberries.

I prune them when needed and pick them as they ripen. It is always good to see the red berry emerging beside the green leaf: they make a fine pair. I grow them for a reason: I grow them for you.

> Some offer juniper,
> Others mimosa;
> I am the bringer of raspberries.

Elegua—Eshu in the Yoruba religion—is the deity of gateways, roads and messages in Lukumí belief. His counterpart in Vodou belief is Papa Legba, who will accept, amongst other flora, a gift of strawberries. (See STRAWBERRY.*)*

ROSE

Rosa spp., qaga, ward, tsistunagiska

A wild rose is a bramble without the berry—indeed, rose hips, though edible and nutritious, are rather poor fare compared to the fruits of rose's cousins: blackberries and raspberries, strawberries, apples, pears, almonds, and stone fruit. But humans have mainly grown roses for their beauty, visual and olfactory.

The Chinese were the first to cultivate the rose, but the oldest surviving petals are from Africa: wreaths of *Rosa* × *richardii*, found in an ancient Egyptian tomb. (The same rose species, along with the native African *R. abyssinica*, grows to this day in the church forests of Ethiopia.) In Roman times, Egypt produced unguents for the Empire and shipped petals to Italy for its May festivals of flora. During the medieval period, gardeners in al-Andalus (Muslim Spain) grew and developed an unmatched variety of roses; Muslim agronomists mention climbing roses, yellow roses, and *R. gallica*, which becomes more fragrant when dried.

The Old World flower arrived in America with Spanish colonizers; in one version of the tale of the Virgin of Guadalupe, the Chichimec peasant Juan Diego Cuauhtlatoatzin finds himself in what he takes to be *Xochitlalpan*, his ancestors' land of flowers—but turns out to be a garden of "Castilian" roses.

Yet the flower's less virginal and less European associations persist. In Umbanda and Quimbanda, Pomba Gira of the [Seven] Roses is a notably voluptuous avatar of the sexual, cackling, chainsmoking pomba giras, female counterparts of the exus (Eshu); red roses are used to call upon her power. In Lukumí, roses belong to Oshun.

Tale of a Rose

Jah Folk sat in Papine Square, greeting one and all, while discussion ensued about a *Gleaner* article reporting that a stepmother had imprisoned her young stepdaughter for a few hours over a false accusation. Conversation developed, with people sharing anecdotes, shouting, cursing. To ease down the atmosphere, Jah Folk began to tell a story from Cuba; and he began the tale with a chant of his. The fire withdrew and the heat diminished as his voice came in like a cooling breeze.

> It is me,
> Your sister Marcelita.
> Imprisoned here
> By our stepmother.
> I will survive,
> Becoming a rose:
> Please don't pick me, my brother.

Marcelita becomes an easy scapegoat. I mean, who's going to believe that a bird the color of indigo, with golden wings, took the fig from the treasured tree? So her stepmother, Nicolasa, shoves her in a hole, imprisoning her with a boulder.

Many have had their own encounter with false allegation and its consequences. So the trickery of the stepmother generated jeers and boos. Jah Folk grinned, enjoying our interaction with the tale.

Hearing the song, her brother Manolito runs to his father. Faced with the facts in front of all, Nicolasa confesses and rolls away the boulder. The kidnapped one emerges! Joy returns to the hearth, as daughter, father, and son embrace each other, shedding tears of happiness and relief. Nicolasa is forgiven.

Cheers and whistling were heard from the listeners, and once again, laughter visited the visage of the folklorist. Jah Folk posed a question: How could she be human in the cave and an icon of flora outside of it? And the riddle went back and forth, as good riddles should, but no one could come up with the answer. It transpired that as she was being pushed into the hole, a hair of hers fell outside of it and blossomed into a rose.

Then he taught us the words of a chant, which we sang heartily before we went our separate ways, because everyone wants to be a rescuer rather than a victim, and most of us have a beloved sister or brother.

It is me,
Your brother Manolito.
I'll rescue you
From the evil grotto.
Then, I'll meet you
At reunion junction.
It is time for us to go.

ROSE APPLE

Syzygium jambos, jambo branco, jamrosat, pomarrosa

Rose apples are the fruit of a tall flowering tree in the same genus as the clove and the "java plum" or jambolan. Its flowers look like those of its more distant relative the eucalyptus, but larger, with more flamboyant stamens. The fruits, when ripe, smell floral and resemble guavas—on the outside, that is, since on the inside they have a firm yellow flesh that contains only two seeds.

The rose apple tree is native to Southeast Asia. Portuguese colonists brought it to Brazil in the mid-18th century, and from there it became established in the Caribbean. It was long regarded as invasive there, but the rose apple's vulnerability to guava rust disease has brought its population under control. The tree has also naturalized in parts of West Africa and on islands like Zanzibar that have long had trade connections with its place of origin.

The rose apple is adored by bees and children. It can be eaten raw; in Guyana, it is also made into a kind of lemonade. In Brazil, it is associated with the orisha Oxalá (Obatala.)

Tale of Rose Apple

Did you ever see a duppy turn green?
Green, green,
Like a runner bean:
Too many rose apples.

Did you ever see a duppy change color?
Holler, holler
For nurse or doctor:
Bingeing on rose apples.

Did you ever see a duppy cry?
Cry, cry
Into the river and die:
Rose apple gluttony.

And that's how Jah Folk began the tale about Pickwa and the Duppy. You should have heard the gentle hullabaloo in Papine Square in the discussion about duppies; everyone had a story to tell and wanted to share it! For a little while, the square became a location for improvisation as individuals acted out certain episodes. A family duppy, Rolling Calf, obeah man, anecdote of a friend, the Rose Hall witch, movements in the night, Ol' Higue, sounds from the blackness, shivers down the spine, and sensations across the face! Gesticulations enhanced the telling as we saw reenactments of the frightened ones' moments of horror. If Carl Bradshaw had been there, he would have been impressed with some of the dramatical skills on display. It was street theater at its very best. There was agreement and disagreement, touching of fists and turning of backs—playfully—as vignettes went around and comedy illuminated the Kingston night, a festival of humor in Papine Square.

As time was moving on, Jah Folk steered the conversation back around to the subject of excess. Continuing the tale from Jamaica that he'd begun with the three verses, he tells us of a boy called Pickwa, who is up in a tree and is asked to abandon the best-looking rose apple because the overweight duppy below him demands it. Rather than give up his reward, he offers other ones, lots of them... and the expanding phantom accepts them all. Engaging the trickery of Anansi, Pickwa says to the duppy that he'll get the medic he is hollering for so he can descend from the treetop snare. Once he's back on the ground, he runs—but not to the house of the doctor, no: he runs home. Arriving there, gasping, sweating, he relays the episode to his mother, who begins to make his favorite pie from the prize-winning rose apple. Meanwhile, the duppy, due to his new rotundity, rolls away into the river to his death.

We laughed at the story. Then Jah Folk led us in a discussion about gluttony. We spoke of all its varieties, such as culinary, sexual, religious, and drug-related. From childhood, we'd all been told that too much of one thing is not a good thing.

He went back to the story, talking of rose apple gluttony. He said, "Just as the colors in my crown, so let them be on your plate: the red of tomato, gold of pumpkin, green of callaloo. Eat well, eat widely. Let all the colors be there on the plate of the evening meal. Put a rainbow inside you every day and feel better for it."

We've had some great nights in Papine Square listening to Jah Folk. That was one of the legendary ones. As on many nights before, we stood and applauded him as he stood and bowed to us. He was ours.

Then the sound came back in full blast as a white taxi and a yellow bus played another round of call-and-response with the tooting of their horns.

ROSEMARY

romero, *Salvia rosmarinus* syn. *Rosmarinus officinalis*, alecrim, romarin, ewere, sawee

Rosemary is a shrub with fragrant, needlelike leaves and bluish flowers. It belongs to the same family as many other great herbs: sage, mint, basil, thyme, perilla or shiso, oregano, and catnip. It prefers a Mediterranean climate, near the sea, but can make its home in a variety of places, including subtropical South Brazil. Ancient Egyptians used rosemary in the embalming process, and the flowering tops of the herb were distilled to make Queen of Hungry Water, for centuries the most popular perfume and cure-all in Europe.

The herb is popular in the African diasporic religions of Candomblé and Umbanda. Practitioners might use rosemary in leaf baths (*amaci*); the leaves are kneaded in cool water, which is then poured the water over the head of the patient. While strong herbs like RUE and CLOVES cleanse the patient of negative energies, sweeter ones like rosemary attract prosperity, happiness, and love. Rosemary can also serve as a concentration and memory aid and a remedy for headaches. In parts of the Caribbean, the name rosemary or wild rosemary can refer to *Croton linearis*, a very similar shrub, the leaves of which may be burned to ward off duppies (ghosts.)

Rosemary is associated with many orishas, particularly the hunter Oxóssi (Oshosi) but both rosemary and cinnamon may be used in the baths of Oshun, orisha of love.

Rosemary and Cinnamon Chant

I want this to work,
Feel she's the one for me:
Bathe me in rosemary.

Wishing for her,
I don't pray for money:
Bathe me in rosemary;
Addition of cinnamon,
And a little sprinkle of cloves.

All's bright and clear,
There's no mystery;
Bathe me in rosemary.

Just her and I
And eternity:
Bathe me in rosemary;
Addition of cinnamon,
And a little sprinkle of cloves.

RUBBER TREE

seringueira, *Hevea brasiliensis*, arbol del caucho, arbre a caoutchouc

The rubber tree has ovate, deciduous leaves and can grow up to 150 feet high in the wild. On plantations, which is where the majority of rubber trees in the world can be found, it rarely reaches half this height because of overcrowding and because constant tapping stunts its growth. The tree is tapped for its latex, an immune secretion that dries to form rubber, a substance with elastic and waterproofing properties unrivaled among other natural products.

Native to the Amazon, the rubber tree has been used for millennia by Indigenous people to make clothing, toys, and medical devices. European interest in rubber is more recent, but has led to the enslavement of Indigenous populations in the Amazon and to the growth of rubber plantations. By stealing seeds, the British transplanted the rubber tree to South Asia. It now thrives there even as fungal blights have devastated monocrop rubber plantations in South America.

Mesoamerican cultures from the Olmecs onward used latex derived from a different tree to make the balls used to play the Mexican Ball Game (Nahuatl *ollamaliztli*). Rubber technology was thus widespread in the New World, but completely new to the first Europeans who encountered it. One of the first Spaniards to see a rubber bouncing ball reports suspecting that it was alive.

Rubber Tree Curiosity

Have you ever eaten tapir, smoked? As a vegetarian, I'll never have that experience, but I mention it because that's how this tale begins.

You see, a solitary man goes out tapping rubber one day, returning to find tapir, smoked and waiting for him. How can that be, for a man living without a partner or friend? After his eyeballs return to their sockets and his lower jaw resumes its usual posture, he grins throughout the meal, the happiest of all diners that evening. He sleeps very well that night, awaking to resume his tapping. Returning that evening, he finds another smoked blessing, and his pondering reaches the next level—especially when he sees the words, "Humans don't know what trees know," carved in wood in front of his home. And this is where the old saying, "Curiosity killed the cat," comes in. I say that because, like most of us, he needs to find out who's begun to leave the evening bounty—a natural response to the situation, I think.

So the next day, he concludes the tapping earlier than usual and hides behind a tree. Soon, stepping out from another tree, is a woman clad in bark, who begins to inflame the fire by fanning it with a bird, which she then releases. The magical one senses the watcher. So as soon as

he steps from behind the reconnaissance tree, she disap-
pears. She reappears to him some time later in a dream,
asking him why he could not have been content with what
was provided rather than trying to investigate the source.

A tough lesson! I felt for the solitary man, as I would
have been seriously curious also. Not being able to afford
a private detective, I would have utilized the same meth-
odology. After all, how was he to know he'd encounter the
one called Seringa, Mother of the Rubber Trees? Because
of his misadventure with detection, the trees began to give
less latex. So he had to uproot and move on.

RUE

arruda, ruda, herb-of-grace, *Ruta graveolens* or *chalepensis*

If you've ever taken part in the Ethiopian coffee ceremony, your cup may have come graced with the delicate sprig of a plant. That plant is rue, or, in Amharic, *t'ena'adam*, "Adam's health"—a name that speaks to the antiquity of the herb's use as medicine. The herb is an ingredient in the world's two oldest known cookbooks as well as in the oldest book of herbal medicine, Dioscorides' *De materia medica*.

Rue's popularity has waned in European cookery and medicine owing to safety fears. But in much of the world, rue still holds sway in the kitchen and apothecary. In Ethiopia it adds its musky pungency not just to coffee but to cheese and berbere spice. Soon after rue's arrival with the colonists, Indigenous Americans discovered its many uses, from aiding reproductive health to combatting inflammation. In modern curanderismo rue can feature in *limpias*, spiritual cleansings. Lukumí and Palo practitioners might grow rue on the patio to protect against dark spirits called *ndoki*. In Candomblé and Umbanda, rue is employed in baths as a cleansing herb and for protection, in an amulet called a patuá that wards off the evil eye (a use of rue throughout Europe and the Near East too.)

On Día de la Pachamama, August 1st, Indigenous peoples of the Andes celebrate the Earth Mother and drink a beverage of *caña y ruda*, sugarcane and rue, for health and luck in the coming year.

Arruda Necessity

She loved to share; she gave of her time, creativity and knowledge; she was our symbol of wisdom. Solomon was in the running also, but Mama Solace took the gold. She would share snapshots from her life as props for ours. Out of respect for her privacy, we never delved in too much, but were grateful for the pieces of her soul that she gave to us.

Palmira had come into her compound that day, trembling, after being caught in domestic crossfire. So, looking in her box of reflections, Mama Solace gave us a poem from her mid-teens, when she'd first begun to explore African spirituality and its relation to flora...

Please forgive the intrusion, Ossâim, but may I pass through?
I'm in need of Ruta graveolens, known as arruda or rue.
Tell me, is it best to pick it early morning, or late evening?
Should I wait till the moon is full?

Teacher told us that it's also called "herb of grace," because branches of rue are dipped in sanctified water, which is then sprinkled over the penitent. But no one told me there would be days like these, when parents become Public Enemy Number One to each other; no one told me that cussing and swearing at high volume would become the soundtrack of my childhood. Like Butterfly, but for different reasons, I need this plant: to counteract the aura of tension.

Tell me, Ossâim, wise man of the forest, where and when should I harvest arruda?

Then she regaled us with stories of the guardians of the forest, such as Gronmama in Suriname, who lives in a star apple tree, and the Konderongs of the Gambia, who prefer residence in a baobab.

And so time passed and Palmira smiled again, as we sat under the mango tree, drinking sorrel and giving thanks.

SAFU

elumi, nsafu, atanga, butterfruit, safoutier, *Dacryodes edulis*, ube, butterfruit, African pear, bush mango

Safu is the fruit of a medium-sized tree with large, glossy leaves and a trunk dotted with teardrops of resin. It grows in sub-Saharan West Africa from Liberia to Angola. The fruit itself is dark blue or violet in color, oblong, with a shiny skin; inside, it looks a bit like an avocado, with lime-green flesh surrounding a large pit. The fruit's lipid content is astoundingly high (hence its English name, butterfruit), and its overall nutritional profile is not unlike that of milk or eggs.

Unlike many tropical fruit trees, safu has a reputation for being difficult to propagate and has not been turned into a cash crop, either in Africa or elsewhere in the world. But in its natural range, it is a major agroforestry product. Some people gather safu from the wild, while others grow the trees in gardens or in circular groves with other fruit trees. It is always spared when a field is burned, and can serve as a source of shade in coffee or cocoa plantations. In a domestic setting, the tree's dropped leaves and excess fruit help keep soils fertile.

For farmers in Southern Nigeria, the budding of the safu trees heralds the arrival of planting season. By August, when the fruit is ripe, so is the corn, and both are often eaten together—boiled or roasted over the embers and sprinkled with salt, as the heroine Mbombe preferred.

Tale of Safu

Throughout the year, Jah Folk came into Papine High to help the school celebrate this and that. He still steps in, teaching my son and his peers. My son came home the other day talking of Women's Day celebrations and our generation-bridging man, who taught, using a dialogue, about a Mongo heroine and her time of pregnancy.

RUBY: Excuse me, midwife. Can I ask you if you have had children?

NURSE: Yes, of course you can. I have three: two girls and a boy.

RUBY: Are they well?

NURSE: Yes, giving thanks, they are very well.

RUBY: Ah, that's good to hear. Did you have any cravings?

NURSE: Eh! Don't start me talking! Had cravings during all of them, but the first pregnancy I remember the most.

RUBY: Why's that?

NURSE: Because with Ruby and Amy, I craved different things, but with Robbie, all I wanted was honey! Believe me when I tell you, mother-to-be, that I ate more honey in those nine months than a Maasai woman eats in her whole life! Honey with everything! On toast, plantain, yogurt, crackers, fish: everything. My partner became my honeyguide bird.

RUBY: Ahh, your daughter and I share the same name: I'm Ruby also. Anyway, you can't get enough honey! That's the good stuff. Reminds me of a folktale from the Congo. In fact, let me tell you something, nurse. This time last year, I had just finished my degree. I was easing out, spending time with my good friend, Sonia, talking and laughing. I remember we had a conversation about the blue lotus from the ancient Egyptian stories and about her long-suffering boyfriend Marlon. And a year later, I'm easing my mind into the first months of pregnancy.

NURSE: That's life, little sister. And you've got all those stories to share with the one to come. Yes! I tell you what, the first time the little one falls asleep on your chest, it will make you cry: the sweetest tears you'll ever shed.

RUBY: Ahhh!

NURSE: So tell me this story from the Congo.

RUBY: Yes. So one time the champion wrestler of the Mongo people, a woman named Mbombe, is pregnant; she craves safu nuts. Before her husband can get them for her, she sings to a hornbill, who brings them to her. And like honey, safu is a facilitator of better health. It contains vitamins A and C and other enhancers, like potassium and calcium. It's the original purple pill!

NURSE: My craving, also known as medicine, came in gold. Manuka! They brought me manuka. Because I was pregnant, they said I had to have the best honey: either of local production or manuka. I felt like the queen of the land of sweet things. The midwife and hospital staff began calling me the Honey Whisperer.

RUBY: Well, like Mbombe of the Mongo folktale, your craving brought potential for good health.

NURSE: And on that note, I must leave you.

RUBY: It was good to speak with you; thank you. Take care, Honey Whisperer.

NURSE: It was good to speak with you too, mother-to-be, or shall I call you Mama Griot.

RUBY: Bless you.

NURSE: And bless you—and the little one that is coming.

My son said that following the dialogue—which two female teachers read—Jah Folk facilitated a discussion about cravings, generating surprise and laughter as some of the teachers with children shared their culinary urges during pregnancy—for peanut butter, tuna fish, milk, ginger, chicken, and so on! My son came in, bubbling, saying it was one of the best workshops by a visiting speaker; then, he went to ask his mum what cravings she had when he was inside her belly.

SARSAPARILLA

Smilax ornata, zarzaparilla, japecanga, sachpawè

In the Jamaican tradition of Roots Tonic, knowledgeable people—often Rastafari elders—go into the forest in the days when the moon is fullest to collect bark, roots, and vines. Then they dry and boil these ingredients and allow them to cure or ferment, yielding a drink that imparts strength and vitality. Over two hundred plant species have been recorded as possible ingredients in Roots Tonic, but the power duo of CHANEY ROOT and sarsaparilla is foundational in every formulation.

The word "sarsaparilla" derives from the Spanish *zarza*, "bramble" or "prickle," and *parrilla*, "small grapevine." Indeed, the plant is a thorny vine belonging to the greenbrier family, whose members are found throughout the world, including in North America (though the "wild sarsaparilla" of the eastern US is an unrelated species.) Along with the now-banned sassafras root, the root of *Smilax ornata* was used in the original root beer. A related species features in the Cuban drink called *pru*.

For a time, Jamaican sarsaparilla eclipsed China root in popularity as a medicine in Europe, with Britain importing 345,000 tons a year by the late 19th century, although modern studies show the species' phytochemical properties to be identical.

The plant belongs to Babalú-Ayé, orisha of disease and healing.

Like Sly and Robbie

Like Sly and Robbie,
Saltfish and ackee,
Sarsaparilla and me,
Always working together.

Like Family and Carly,
Rice and peas,
Sarsaparilla and me,
We come in tandem.

Like Santa and Fully,
Ice cream and naseberry,
Sarsaparilla and me:
Epitome of duet.

This is a companion piece to "Chaney Root Chant," celebrating Roots Tonic; Chaney speaks of his relationship with another root, Sarsaparilla. Sly and Robbie, Family and Carly (The Wailers) and Fully and Santa (Soul Syndicate) are three of the great bass and drum teams of roots reggae music. Naseberry, also known as sapodilla, is a fruit popular in the Caribbean.

SHEA

shi, ghariti, karité,
Vitellaria paradoxa

Shea butter comes from a long-lived tree that is slow to mature and outwardly resembles an English oak. The fruits that ripen and fall from these trees are gathered during the rainy season—June to September in the parts of the African Sahel and Savannah where they grow. The process of turning these fruits into shea butter is complex and labor-intensive, beginning with manual separation of the worthless pulp from the valuable nuts and ending, eventually, with the grinding of the nuts to extract the butter. Traditionally, every stage of this work is carried out by women.

Shea butter has been manu-factured in the region since at least 100 CE. It is a treasured gift, offered at births and weddings and to show gratitude for acts of kindness. Shea butter is employed as a lamp oil, for skin care (a use that has caught on globally), medicinally to treat arthritis or joint pain, and in soapmak-ing. It may be offered to the orisha Obatala; it is white, his favorite color.

This piece invokes the role of shea in the creation story of the Bamana of Mali; shea is also sacred to the Acholi, a Nilotic people of Uganda.

The Shea Chant

Tell me of Creation, Bamana Man, aeons before Segu and
Kaarta. Of Pemba and Faro, the two spirits that brought us
into being. Talk to me of acacia.

(*chanted*)
Shea tree,
I beg you come shower me
With the blessings that you give:
Presentations of butter and oil.

So bring the kora, storyteller; the log has begun to burn
and the moon has arrived. Tell me of the first food and the
offerings that were made to the tree of original sustenance.
Talk to me of shea.

(*chanted*)
Shea tree,
I beg you come shower me
With the blessings that you give:
Presentations for food and skincare.

*The Bamana or Bambara – founders of the Segu and Kaarta kingdoms in Mali – are
part of the Mande peoples, found throughout parts of West Africa. Pemba and Faro are
the two spirits of their Creation story.*

SORGHUM

maishi chikí, great millet, broom corn, *Sorghum bicolor*, imphee, durra, jowar, milo, adaza, zahina

From the neck down, Sorghum bicolor looks like corn; from the neck up, it looks like sumac berries. This deep-rooted grass was domesticated thousands of years ago in the region of modern-day South Sudan to become the most drought-resistant of any cereal crop. Sorghum diversified as it spread within Africa (kafir for dry climates and guinea corn for wet ones) and outside of it (durra, the cultivar grown in India). Today, sorghum is the dietary staple of nearly half a billion people.

Enslaved Africans brought sorghum to the plantations of the Caribbean, where they grew it among nitrogen-fixing crops like black-eyed peas. It was also grown as fallow in the sugarcane fields. The crop was well adapted for Caribbean climates Sorghum stalks can be pounded and boiled into a molasses-like syrup, dried as a spice, or used for thatching. The seeds can be ground into a flour, roasted whole, or fermented into beer. Sorghum beer was ceremonially important in the ancient African kingdoms of Kush and Meroë, and it continues to play a role in the ritual life of peoples across the continent.

In Jamaica, sorghum is known for its ability to ward off the shapeshifting hags called soucouyants. On arid Bonaire off the coast of Venezuela, sorghum grows on *kunuku* farms (Taíno: *conuco*) and goes into the island's signature kadushi cactus liqueur. During the months of the sorghum harvest, each *kunuku* celebrates with processions, song, and dance.

Sorghum Pancake

I know you've heard of earthquake, but what about mirth-quake? The tremors of laughter as humor goes rumbling through the streets!

In Bonaire, every year between February and April is mirthquake season, when they celebrate Simadan, the harvest of sorghum. Bonaire becomes the epicenter of joy, people enjoying each successive wave of it, relishing each shudder of quake; dancing *wapa*, eating *repa*: blessings of Sorghum Pancake.

In the Papiamentu language of Bonaire, wapa is a communal dance; repa is sorghum pancake.

SOURSOP

wanaban, guanábana, graviola, kowosol, cachiman, *Annona muricata* ebom, eko omonde, abo, apa oka

The soursop is a mid-sized tree with peculiar fruits, green and spiky, that grow up to a foot long in a bulbous bean shape. The tree belongs to the *Annona* genus along with several species that bear similar fruits, including custard-apple or sweetsop and cherimoya, both similar in appearance but scaly-looking rather than prickly. All produce fruit from large yellow flowers, which are fleshy like those of their cousins the magnolias (whose pods in turn resemble small tough soursops) and likewise beetle-pollinated. The fruit's texture is creamy, tasting of apple and strawberries along with a sour citrus note that gives the fruit its English name, and it makes a delicious ice cream flavor.

Soursop is one of the trees, like STARAPPLE, PAPAYA, and GUAVA, that grew in the gardens of the Taíno people; the Spanish name, guanábana, comes from the Taíno wanaban. In today's Caribbean, the tree grows alongside citrus and calabash trees in the middle canopy layer of "creole gardens" or food forests. It's now joined its indigenous sibling *A. senegalensis* in West Africa and spread to India and Southeast Asia. Most parts of the plant, particularly the leaves and bark, have medicinal value, although the toxic seeds are perhaps most useful as an insecticide.

Soursop is the favorite fruit of Obatala in the Lukumí tradition; it can also be offered to Babalú-Ayé, the twin orishas the Ibejis, and to Orishaoko (Oko.)

Discourse of Soursop and Sage

One night, Jah Folk took us from Papine Square across the water, to where they sing Santería. He took us back to ancient belief, aeons before the coming of those represented by the cross or by the crescent. Via Cuba, we went back to Africa, to the altar of original praise. Rastaman spoke with us of Obatala. Talking of the flora associated with him, the offerings. Now and again during those Papine evenings, Jah Folk would read something he'd written, and this is what he read with a neighbor of his on that night, the song of a fruit and a herb...

SOURSOP: Time again, old friend.

SAGE: Yes my friend, time 'gain to serve.

SOURSOP: To where they chant Obatala.

SAGE: The one who molded them.

SOURSOP: Deity of their creation.

SAGE: Festivity in white.

SOURSOP: Celebration without booze.

SAGE: Yes, the forbidden substance. I guess all the crew will be there.

SOURSOP: I expect so.

SAGE: Pomegranate.

SOURSOP: Coconut.

SAGE: Yes, coconut. An offering to other orishas also.

SOURSOP: Fruit of their divination, when four pieces of it are thrown.

SAGE: Yes, they call it Obi. So who else will attend?

SOURSOP: Acacia's usually there.

SAGE: Yes. And rice.

SAGE: Of course, Obatala loves rice pudding.

SOURSOP: His all-time favorite, I think.

SAGE: Yes, I think it may top his list.

SOURSOP: Yam.

SAGE: Alfalfa.

SOURSOP: Garlic.

SAGE: Yes, but not salt.

SOURSOP: No, never salt.

SAGE: Hawthorn.

SOURSOP: Parsley.

SAGE: I'm sure there are a few others, but can't think of them right now.

SOURSOP: That's the thing, because we're all there up against each other, it's hard to see who's who sometimes!

SAGE: Anyway, you and I are ready to fulfill the sacred duty.

SOURSOP: Soursop and Sage, ever ready to help the humans pay homage to Creation.

In some versions of the Yoruba creation story, Obatala is said to be the one who facilitated Earth's creation; other versions say it was Oduduwa.

STAR APPLE

sterappel, estrella, goldenleaf tree, abyaba, pomme surette, *Chrysophyllum cainito*

The star apple tree is one of the *Sapotaceae*, a family of tropical fruit-bearing trees beloved wherever they grow but, with a few exceptions, little known elsewhere. The family name is derived from "tzapotl," the Nahuatl word for a member of the family also known as sapote, sapodilla, and naseberry (*Manilkara zapota*.) Others in the family include mamey sapote, lúcuma, abiu, udara (*Gambeya* spp., a West African tree sometimes also called star apple), argan, and SHEA.

The star apple's deep purple fruits, about the size of ordinary apples, are so called because when sliced in half latitudinally the seeds form a many-pointed starburst. The tree's genus, *Chrysophyllum* and common name "goldenleaf tree" allude to the hue of the leaves' velvety underside. Because of the leaf's two faces, hypocrites are called *caimitos* in Caribbean

idiom, and the plant is used to work concealment magic in Palo Mayombe practice.

The fruit's peel and rind contain a sticky, mildly toxic latex, so the juicy pulp must be scooped out. It is often used to top ice cream, or, in Jamaica, mixed with citrus and condensed milk to make a fruit salad called matrimony.

The tree was likely first domesticated in Panama or the Antilles and grows carefree throughout Central America and the Caribbean. It's been planted in gardens and streetside in tropics from Sri Lanka to the Philippines. The Haitian revolutionary general Henri Christophe, later king, held court under a star apple that two hundred years later still stands outside his former palace. In Suriname, the star apple is the residence of the spirit Gronmama—Green Mother.

Star Apple Chant

GRONMAMA
Harm does not breed here,
So come with respect,
I live in this star apple tree.

VOICES
Some say Sterappel,
Others Estrella.

GRONMAMA
I am Gronmama.

VOICES
She watches over the land,
All along Suriname River,
Through every tributary.

GRONMAMA
Bedecked in purple,
A splash of green:
Go easy when you're passing me.

VOICES
Called her Purple Star
And Golden Leaf.

GRONMAMA
I am Mother Earth.

VOICES
She watches over the land,
All along Suriname River,
Through every tributary.

For Frits Van Toorn

In the Creole orality of Suriname, performances often begin with a song in tribute to Gronmama, also known as Aysa, Maysa, and by other monikers.

STRAWBERRY

Fragraria × *ananassa*, fresa, morango, niihontesha

The red aggregate fruits of this creeping, large-leafed plant are a global commodity with a complicated history. Strawberries have always been part of Indigenous cuisine in the Americas. Settlers sent cuttings and seeds of these culinary strawberries back to Europe, where they quickly replaced the small and relatively flavorless varieties that were native there. The modern eating strawberry, *Fragraria* × *ananassa*, is a cross of two American varieties, one from the Eastern US and the other from Chile.

Later, that hybrid came back to the Americas, where it's grown in backyard gardens as well as on massive agribusiness plantations that sometimes overtax local water supplies. The Haudenosaunee still cherish the wild North American strawberry as a sign of summer, celebrating a strawberry festival when the fruits begin to ripen.

Strawberries for Papa Legba

And the aging one, entering his sixth decade, said one day to Papa Legba,

"Although I still ask for guidance, I bring you this presentation not for myself, no; I bring you this calabash of gifts for my two children, as they commence their respective journeys.

"If they should meet someone at Admiration Crossroads and love should develop, let it be real and long. Let them know Fulfillment Road, rather then Wreckage Lane. I hope honesty lights the way, always. Point them in the direction of integrity.

"Let every step between them and their partner be empowered by respect. Don't let them know the wastelands: I hope they're not the cause of it, generating the shadow that never leaves. The solitary trudge, over and over, across the bridge of mangled hope, into the street of the shattered heart; the years of errors, the decades of mess. And if they have to walk down Redemption Road, let it be only once, or not too often. I hope they leave a sweet legacy. I bring you the best of Fragaria,

Papa Legba: please accept this offering of strawberries."

Sitting under the legendary mango tree, Mama Solace told us she'd written this piece a decade or so before, after the passing of a neighbor and friend of hers: a man, who during his lifetime, had found and lost three good women due to his ongoing lack of commitment. She'd seen his days of exuberance and the times of gloom, when he was ashamed to show his face; he, a lover of life and people, transformed into a hermit. Out of all the pieces she shared with us over the decades from her little box of reflections, I think this is the one that resonates the most as I approach middle age.

In the Vodou religion of Haiti, Papa Legba is the gatekeeper and messenger, the loa (spirit) of roads and opportunities. He is the counterpart of the Yoruba orisha, Eshu, also known as Elegua (Lukumí) and Exu (Candomblé and Umbanda). Strawberries are one of the fruits offered to Papa Legba.

SUGARCANE

canne à sucre, *Saccharum officinarum*, caña de azúcar, ireke

Sugarcane is a very tall grass with a thick, fibrous stalk that drips with a sweet-tasting whitish-gray sap when cut. It grows wild in Papua New Guinea and Southeast Asia. Sugarcane was domesticated in that region and grown as a crop in China and India, whence Islamic merchants brought it to the Near East. Europeans began to cultivate sugarcane in the wake of the crusades, and the earliest European settler colonies in the Canary Islands and the Madeiras started off as sugar-growing operations.

When sugar came to the Caribbean, slavery came with it. Sugar was the first New World crop to be produced by slave labor—first, briefly, that of convicts and native peoples, then that of captured Africans. Cultivating sugarcane was, and still is, backbreaking work: from planting stem cuttings to weeding and hoeing the fields to macheteing the mature plants with their razor-sharp leaves, every step of the process is labor intensive—and the work must all be carried out in the tropical heat the plants require.

In the Caribbean, the sugar industry began a slow decline after abolition, but sugarcane is still an important part of Caribbean culture and cuisine. People chew on the stalks and drink the raw syrup or boil it down to make panela or rock candy. The orisha Elegua (Eshu) may be given all of these, while Ochún (Oshun) prefers confectionery. And the Trinidadian festival of Canboulay begins when the cane stalks are set alight in commemoration of the cane harvest. "Canboulay" comes from the French *cannes brûlées*: burnt canes.

Canboulay

Since Abolition,
Canboulay.
Lighting the cane stalks,
Canboulay.
Nighttime procession,
Canboulay.
Masquerade time,
Canboulay.
The drums can be heard,
Canboulay.
Homage to color,
Canboulay.
Dance of victory,
Canboulay.
Chanting heritage,
Canboulay.
Roots of Carnival,
Canboulay.

Carnival began in Christian traditions as a time of indulgence before Lent. The French would hold their carnivals within the grounds of their homes on the island. It was the formerly enslaved who first took Carnival to the streets.

Canboulay was the precursor of Trinidad Carnival as we know it today, which begins with the lighted procession of cane stalks, that item of flora so associated with slavery.

SWEET POTATO

Ipomoea batatas, batata-doce, jetica, kukundunku

The sweet potato plant is related to morning glory. Like morning glory, it grows in a vinous habit and produces attractive, funnel-shaped flowers. The tubers that grow at the base of the plant are a staple food in tropical regions all over the world, including Sub-Saharan Africa. Since it tolerates drought well, gives good nutritional return even on tiny plots, and can be cultivated easily without expensive machinery, the sweet potato is an ideal crop for small-scale farmers to feed their families or take to market.

The sweet potato was domesticated in South America, where the Incas farmed it. Whether by chance or because of contact between the people of South America and those of the islands of the Pacific, sweet potatoes also found their way to Polynesia and Papua New Guinea, where the cultural importance of this crop would be hard to overstate. As Anansi migrated to the Caribbean from Ghana, sweet potato was imported into Africa, part of the Columbian Exchange. In the diaspora, the tuber came to fill many of the same roles as the yam did in Africa. The Portuguese brought it to the coast of West Africa, but formerly enslaved Africans returning from the New World established it as a major crop inland.

Both the tubers and the leaves are a central part of West African cuisine. Sweet potatoes are now even more important in East Africa, where they are dried and ground into flour for a range of uses. Women often tend the sweet potato crop at every stage, from planting to growing to harvest. The sweet potato is one of the offerings that can be presented to Oko, the orisha of agriculture.

Soul of Ipomoea

All I ask is one,
So roast me a sweet potato.
I am the one who says yes
When the rain says no.
Watchman of the soil,
Spirit of agriculture,
I am the one called Oko.

Someone else watches Ant;
I guard the things that grow,
Consoling the farmer
When he receives a blow.
Carer for nutrients,
Soul of *Ipomoea*:
I am the one called Oko.

TAMARIND

Tamarindus indica, tamarinier, tsamiya, koat

The tamarind tree is indigenous to Africa, although its name, shortened from the Arabic *tamar hindi*, means "Indian date"—a testament to tree's long residence on the subcontinent, where it arrived along with baobab as early as 3000 BCE. The trees reached the Antilles and Central America in the sixteenth century. Their seeds germinate readily wherever they fall, and today they line roadsides where wayfarers once tossed the spent fruits. The fruits themselves are like huge, hard peapods; as with JATOBA, the pulp surrounding the seeds—sweet-and-sour and chestnut-colored, in the tamarind's case—is what humans consume, whether in Worcestershire sauce, agua fresca, or pad thai.

In Africa, these tall trees, with feathery foliage like that of their cousins the acacia and flametree, grow in savanna-forest mosaics—often, like jackalberry, atop termite mounds. The tree's dense shade creates a humid atmosphere and stable temperature around the mound. This environment benefits the termites, and the fruits' pulp and shells are a food source for the termites and other animals. In exchange, the termites, and their fungal and bacterial allies, break down nutrients for the trees.

The Nuer of South Sudan say they were originally born from a great tamarind tree, dropping from its branches like the pods do, or emerging from a hole at its root. Tamarind trees are the home of the iskoki spirits in Hausa orality. Across the Atlantic, in Cuban Lukumí practice, tamarind may be offered to the Babalú-Ayé, orisha of illness and health; in Haiti, the tree is a dwelling-place of Gran Bwa, loa of herbs and earth.

Tale of Tamarind

> Time to chant *Tamarindus*,
> Raise my voice for *indica*.

Leaving Hope River after a little meditation and contem‑
plating peanut porridge, Jah Folk is hailed by a group
relaxing in front of Shanty Man, eating and drinking. He
greets them all, salutes the proprietor, who hands him a
bottle of his Roots Juice, a.k.a. Roots Wine. While enjoying
the blend of ginger, sarsaparilla and other enchanting
things, he talks with them of tamarind. And now and again,
when he signals, they join their voices together, chanting
what he has taught them.

> Time to chant *Tamarindus*,
> Raise my voice for *indica*.

He told them of Silamaka, a hero of the Fulani. The
Fulani, the great herders of West Africa, from Senegal to
Chad. They possess great knowledge of cattle and equal
knowledge of books, having produced some of the shin‑
ing scholars of sub‑Saharan Africa, such as Nana Asma'u
and Mohammed al‑Kaburi. Kaburi taught at Timbuktu
University, which had its Golden Age in the 16th century.
That's why they'd hailed Jah Folk: there's always some‑

thing to learn from him, shared in that easy, interactive manner he has. People passing in vehicles—cars, motor-bikes, and trucks—bib their horns at the gathering that is growing, and those walking up and down Gordon Town Road stop awhile. Soon everyone's giving their opinion on the the merits of ginger and lime juice in a tamarind drink.

> Time to chant *Tamarindus*,
> Raise my voice for *indica*.

Like some people go to a diviner, medium, or pastor, before commencing any venture; so Silamaka, before the time of battle, spends time at the tamarind tree. His tree for thinking and mental preparation, under which his talisman lays. And he'd go there after the battle also, to ease down, to reflect, to rest. Lovely the way Jah Folk put it out there, asking those around him if they had a favorite tree, one they liked to rest their back against. Under which tree would they place their talisman? He made sure everyone had their say; mango, silk cotton and banana appeared to carry group consensus. Then they got into a discussion about whether to add hot pepper or rum to tamarind balls: and that set the people off! While they talk and laugh, he eats a little peanut porridge; then it is time to go. Walking on after the warm farewell, he can hear them, singing of the meditation tree.

> Time to chant *Tamarindus*,
> Raise my voice for *indica*.

TARO

dasheen, cocoyam, inhame, cará, tanya, *Colocasia esculenta*, malanga (isleña)

Taro is a broad-leafed plant often sold as a houseplant, colocasia or "elephant ear," but its edible corm or underground stem has been a staple food in Polynesia since time immemorial. Carried by Austronesian sailors or Red Sea traders, taro landed in Eastern Africa millennia ago. Valued for its ability to grow in places too wet or swampy for other crops, it was cultivated in the Nile Valley and the Mediterranean in antiquity.

In North African and Arab cooking, taro may have been supplanted by potatoes, which are easier to grow and prepare. Taro cultivation is hard work, since plants have to be earthed up continuously to encourage growth. The corm is toxic unless cooked well, and the edible leaves also need careful preparation.

In the Caribbean, taro was one of the foundational crops that enslaved people grew on the provision grounds of plantations, having brought it with them from Africa. Smaller taro tubers are called eddoes; those with larger ones, dasheen, a name that comes via Creole from the French "chou de Chine," "Chinese cabbage." Taro shares many other names with the very similar *Xanthosoma sagittifolium*, yautía. The leaves of both plants can be used in callaloo, the classic Caribbean dish of greens (themselves also sometimes called callaloo.) There are as many versions of callaloo as there are islands, but in the callaloo that is Dominica's national dish, dasheen is the key.

Day of Dasheen

Some call me Dasheen, others Taro. And some have extended the two syllables to nine: *Colocasia esculenta*. However they wish to label me, once a year, everyone comes together, enjoying a culinary wonder in which I am the central feature.

(*chanted*)
Taro, Taro,
Happy festival flow,
Celebrating Creole Day.

They dance and dance, like I do when Breeze decides she needs a choreography partner. They dance and dance. The women in floral skirts, the men in checked waistcoats. And when they have finished the step and the twirl, they enjoy me in a dish. Well, not always me, as some prefer another member of the Green Leaf Crew, my old friend Spinach. Whether its he or I, we are integral to Callaloo Soup.

(*chanted*)
Callaloo, Callaloo,
Enough there for me and you,
Celebrating Creole Day.

Bubbling away, interacting with crab, coconut milk, green banana, cornmeal dumpling, chives, parsley, thyme and pimento; served with slices of avocado. Every year, on the last Friday of October, they honor heritage with me.

(*chanted*)
Dasheen, Dasheen
I'm the Green Leaf Queen,
Celebrating Creole Day.

TOBACCO

Nicotiana tabacum, tabac, joeli, semah, picietl

The tobacco plant has thin stems, broad leaves, and delicate yellow flowers that could, if you squint, remind you of the flowers of tomato or tomatillo, its relatives in the solanum family. Tobacco leaves have been dried and smoked for a long time, at least since 1500 BCE in Mesoamerica. By the fifteenth century, tobacco was being culti-vated all over North America, where people used it as a trade item and a social lubricant.

The European settlers liked it for similar purposes, and they established slave-driven tobacco plantations throughout the Caribbean. In Cuba, Puerto Rico, and the Dominican Republic, tobacco stood its ground against the more profitable SUGARCANE and remains an important part of agriculture on those islands today. Grown from seeds or from starts, tobacco is also an important crop for small farmers.

In the Americas, tobacco has long been one of the plants of the most ceremonial importance. In a liquid or as a powder, Mexica healers have used tobacco to fumigate, to induce visions, and to ease childbirth. In Lukumí, all the male orishas appreciate being offered tobacco. Elegua (Eshu) is known for his love of cigars, as is his counterpart Papa Legba in Vodou.

242

Hebu

SOLO VOICE
Don't bring him papaya.

VOICES
No, no.

SOLO VOICE
Nor aloe vera.

VOICES
No, no.

SOLO VOICE
If you want to appease him,

VOICES
Don't sing him a hymn:
Bring him a portion of tobacco.

SOLO VOICE
Don't bring him cerasee.

VOICES
No, no.

SOLO VOICE
Neither gooseberry,

VOICES
No, no.

SOLO VOICE
To get on his good side,

VOICES
So thoughts don't collide:
Bring him a portion of tobacco.

SOLO VOICE
Don't bring him callaloo.

VOICES
No, no.

SOLO VOICE
Nor nut of cashew.

VOICES
No, no.

SOLO VOICE
For good interaction,

VOICES
So there's no confusion:
Bring him a portion of tobacco.

TRUMPET TREE

Tecoma stans, Ginger Thomas, yellow cedar, chevalier, tronadora, xcanlol, caballito, kusi urakame, koyawari

Yellow trumpet tree or ginger thomas is a shrub or small tree that blooms nearly year-round. Its yellow bell-shaped flowers are followed by tangles of seed capsules that resemble long flat beans. In its family are other flowering plants of Neotropical origin, including FLAME VINE and jacaranda. Trumpet tree is the national tree of the US Virgin Islands, where it might be found by roadsides or in the lower story of the dry forest, shaded by tamarind.

In humid conditions, trumpet tree acts as a ruderal or pioneer species, the first to arrive in areas that have been disrupted by fire or by human intervention; such species tend to reproduce prolifically, aided by the wind, with seeds that can germinate in a wide range of environments. These capabilities incline the plants to become "invasive" in certain contexts, and indeed trumpet tree is labeled as such in several countries, including South Africa.

In both its its older and newer homes, the plant has something to offer bees, butterflies, hummingbirds, and humans. On the Virgin Islands, the leaves are brewed into a popular "bush tea" to stimulate appetite and lower blood sugar. On the Indian subcontinent, the root is made into an antivenom, a use its name in Yucatecan may also reflect: xcanlol, "flower of the snake." The flowers still grow amid Mayan temples, a link to history.

Trumpet tree is a plant for Oshun, since she loves the color yellow.

Trumpet Tree Ensemble

Tell me, Yellow Trumpet Tree, when Mama Leona passed by, did you play your very best? Did you radiate at your brightest, holder of sunlit instruments? Like the players of ivory horn, in their musical salutes to Queen Mother Idia of Benin. I imagine Mama Leona giving thanks for you, as Oba Esigie gave thanks for his mother.

An ensemble of brass, uniformed in green, playing for the esteemed listener: and I imagine her smiling, clasping her hands in thanks to you. Then she and Saffron Finch get into a call and response, with her leading, and everyone wants to join in— Hummingbird, Butterfly, Warbler, Lizard, and the rest—for another session of the Green and Yellow Festival.

As the Edo sang of Queen Mother Idia, so Crucians chant of Mama Leona. She sang of the ancestors; great to hear you praising her, flower of childhood play and national significance. I think of you always ready, spick and span, highly polished, to render sweet melody for the Golden One from your iridescent songbook. Come, Yellow Trumpet Tree, play the Cariso Concerto for me. And let the lead trumpeter play, on and on, the Mama Leona Eulogy.

A piece from my "Mama Leona Trilogy." Leona Brady Watson is a cultural icon of St. Croix. She was a vocalist and promoter of Cariso music—female voice with drum accompaniment—which dates from the time of enslavement.

UMABOPHE

Mabophe, umayibophe wehlathi, *Acridocarpus natalitius*, motvrug, moth-fruit

Umabophe is a category of plant whose roots work a powerful binding magic, according to many peoples of southern Africa. The particular species identified as *umabophe* varies from region to region and may refer to several different plants. In Pondoland, umabophe most often designates *Acridocarpus natalitius*, known as moth-fruit in English because of its mothlike winged fruits or samaras (the technical term for the "helicopters" or "whirligigs" of maple trees as well.) The plant's growth habit can vary from small tree to liana-like rambling shrub, but it is always recognizable by its leathery evergreen leaves and conical racemes of large golden flowers.

The term "umabophe" comes from the verb *bopha*, "to tie up, arrest, or bring to a halt", common to the related Xhosa, Zulu, and Swati languages; many other plants' local names similarly derive from their medicinal and magical properties. Infusing moth-fruit's red root in water produces a protective medicine known as *intelezi*, which can be sprinkled to avert danger or confuse an enemy. Baboons, associated with the ancestors, were thought to use the plant for similar purposes. In a different practice, the plant is chewed while IBHULU burns on the coals as a combined protective measure against lightning. This practice is called *ukuchila*.

Ukuchila

Hey, golden flower,
May I take from your root?
A storm is about to play.
I'll chew you and spit you
So lightning can't win,
Spitting towards the doorway.

VANILLA

tlilxochitl, *Vanilla planifolia*, fanila,
baunilha

Vanilla beans are the seed pods of a climbing orchid native to the tropical areas of Mexico, where the Mexica used them to make medicinal amulets and to flavor chocolate drinks. The Spanish invaders developed a taste for chocolate too, and when hot chocolate made its way to Europe it brought vanilla along for the ride. Growing demand for vanilla flavor independent of chocolate led to vanilla cultivation in the Caribbean and other parts of the colonized tropics, including Madagascar, whence the vanilla orchid spread to mainland Africa too.

As a plant that needed insect pollination and was picky about its pollinators, vanilla was impossible to mass produce and astronomically expensive. Around 1840, on the island of Reunion, an enslaved 12-year-old boy named Edmond Albius developed a technique for hand-pollinating the orchids that made vanilla cultivation cheaper and more dependable. However, the pods must still be harvested by hand, making vanilla one of the world's most expensive flavors. It can be offered to the orisha Oshun, who delights in the luxurious.

The Vanilla Legacy

Love was there,
But seen as transgression:
Let there be vanilla.

In one of the classic stories of love forbidden, a Totonac prince and princess, without following traditional procedure, especially for the nobility, find a quiet place in the forest. Discovered by the priests, they are killed.

A little while later, a plant begins to grow at the place of this enforced conclusion. And what it exudes is something sweet and wonderful for the nasal system to interact with. It makes the nostrils dance, the grin widen, and the eyes sparkle. Its emanation blesses the whole forest: Quetzal sings a new song, and Butterfly joins in harmony.

And I wonder: on his rounds across the region, did the Rain God Tajín reserve a special showering for the plant of love's memory? Did the Sun God fight the clouds every day to make sure it had light and warmth? And one more question; did the people cry for Zempoala as the lovers cried for each other? I imagine them whispering to each other, blowing kisses, smiling before that encounter with the executioner.

252

Love was taken,
But left a legacy:
Let there be vanilla.

From Mexico comes one of the classic tales of forbidden love in Caribbean folklore. Another is the Legend of the Hummingbird, from Puerto Rico, which tells of the love between an Arawak maiden and a Carib youth.

The Totonac are a people indigenous to the Veracruz region of Mexico. El Tajín is their deity of rain and thunder; an important city, said to have been a spiritual center, carries his name. Another major city was Zempoala. Crying for Zempoala refers to the trauma caused by the smallpox brought by the Spanish, which killed most of its residents.

WATER CABBAGE

oju oro, *Pistia stratiotes*, water lettuce, lechuguilla, alface-d'água

The lettuce- or cabbage-like rosettes of this floating plant are a common sight in lakes and ponds throughout the tropics and subtropics and in fish ponds elsewhere. The colonial explorer William Bartram found his attempts to cross lakes foiled by dense mats of water cabbage; like succulents and strawberries, the plants spawn themselves in miniature many times over in the form of offsets or "pups" and spread quickly. Though historically "native" to all most continents, water cabbage can behave invasively wherever it lives, its roots twining together to form the impassable mats. Sometimes, these mats turn the water below anoxic and cause fish to die; they can also host bacteria and mosquitoes.

But water cabbage is also an alchemist: it takes up nutrients like potassium from the water, making it useful as fertilizer as well as in cases where too many nutrients have caused eutrophication. Water cabbage also draws contaminants from the water, purifying it. Because it contains mineral salts (mainly potassium chloride), ash from the burned plant has long been used as a condiment in place of table salt. These minerals also make the ash a valuable ingredient in soap.

In Orisha belief, water cabbage, along with the white lotus (osibata), represents kingship (it "crowns" the water) and victory, since it floats above the unpredictable current of events. Fittingly, it is the item for the student during exam time. As a freshwater plant, it belongs to the orisha Oshun.

Chant Oju Oro

SOLO VOICE
Floating on the water,

VOICES
Oju Oro for Ruby.

SOLO VOICE
Known as Water Cabbage,

VOICES
Oju Oro for Ruby.

SOLO VOICE
Aquatic talisman,

VOICES
Oju Oro for Ruby.

SOLO VOICE
Dry and pound the leaves,

VOICES
Oju Oro for Ruby.

SOLO VOICE
Mix the powder with honey,

VOICES
Oju Oro for Ruby.

SOLO VOICE
Invocation time,

VOICES
Oju Oro for Ruby.

SOLO VOICE
At university,

VOICES
Oju Oro for Ruby.

SOLO VOICE
Worcester College, Oxford,

VOICES
Oju Oro for Ruby.

SOLO VOICE
Success in her exams,

VOICES
Oju Oro for Ruby.

SOLO VOICE
She'll leave with a degree,

VOICES
Oju Oro for Ruby.

For my daughter, Ruby Duncan

WATERMELON

tsamma, xaal w'i, egusi baara, *Citrullus lanatus*, agbeye, melancia, sandía

Like many of their cucurbit kin, the original watermelons were bitter. Native to Africa, they were depicted in paintings in pharaoh's tombs, and the seeds have been found in their tombs as well. Ancient Africans selected the fruit not only for sweetness and high water content—so crucial in the desert—but also for its seeds, which may be used to thicken and flavor egusi, a stew thick like gumbo. In African agriculture, different types of watermelon are often grown side by side to preserve genetic diversity, and the seeds may be sown in the same hole as sorghum or millet to help shade out weeds.

Enslaved Africans brought watermelons to the western hemisphere, grew them in the provision grounds of planta' tions and Maroon communities, and developed improved varieties of the fruit. The melons initially appealed to white Americans' tastes. But after Emancipa' tion, former enslavers began to see in the watermelon, as in the carefree PUMPKIN, a crop whose economy repudiated the planta' tion's—in this case grown with African agricultural expertise, for Black enjoyment and profit—and attached to it racist tropes. By this time the popular fruits had spread: on Native American trade routes, to be grown by Hopi in the high desert and by Kickapoo beside the Great Lakes; to Mexico, to be made into agua fresca and adorn Lotería card 28; and throughout the US, to be eaten in peak season on Independence Day.

Watermelon is among the gifts that can be presented to the orisha Yemanjá (Yemoja), who presides over the deep ocean, at the festival in her honor in Bahia, Brazil—the area of Brazil home to the most people of African descent.

Watermelon Gift

Going down to the beach,
Come along with me,
Time to float watermelon.
Some bring pineapple,
Some coconut;
We shall offer watermelon.

Watch over the young sailor, Yemoja, who holds the latest love letter to his chest. Watch over the old fisherman who blows kisses to his grandchildren. Defend the coastline against invasion by hunger. Immerse every child in the aroma of laughter; and we shall bring gifts of gratitude and drum and dance for you.

YAM

ñambi, isu, kwi,
ñame, inhame,
Dioscorea alata

Yams are the tubers of any of a number of vine-like plants with heart-shaped leaves in the genus *Dioscorea*. The tubers themselves come in a variety of shapes, sizes, and colors, not to mention that the word "yam" can also refer to unrelated plants like sweet potato (in the US) and taro root (in Brazil).

Yams have been domesticated more than once and at various points on the globe, but the varieties most often farmed for food today (of *D. cayennensis* s.l.) originated in Africa. The name "yam" itself is of African origin. Enslaved Africans brought yams to the Caribbean and planted them on the small allotments of earth that the enslavers gave them with an eye to reducing their own overhead. These provision grounds were often just called yam grounds.

For the Igbo, yams are of deep importance and are under the protection of yam deity Njoki Ji. In Yoruba belief, the orisha of agriculture, Oko, plays a part in making yam tubers grow big and may receive them as an offering at the annual yam festival. Ogun, god of the forge and war, may be offered yams cooked in palm oil. Yams may also be offered to Oduduwa, as here.

Oduduwa Haiku

I bring you a yam,
Facilitator of Earth,
A tuber of thanks.

From Yoruba orality. Commissioned by Oludumore the Creator, aided by a chicken and some soil, Earth was created; some versions say the creation was carried out by Oduduwa, others say Obatala.

YERBA MATE

ka'a, *Ilex paraguariensis*

Yerba mate is a holly plant with a treelike growth habit and leaves that can be steeped in hot or cold water to produce a tasty and caffeinated tea. The tea is traditionally consumed via metal straw from a gourd or other container shared among friends, making yerba drinking an important social ritual in Brazil, Argentina, and other South American countries where yerba mate is a popular stimulant.

The Guaraní and Tupi people, living in what's now Paraguay, were brewing and drinking yerba for centuries before the Spanish arrived. In the wake of the Spanish invasion, the Jesuits were the first Europeans to encounter this beverage and were instrumental in spreading it throughout the continent. To do that, they depended on Indigenous knowledge about how to germinate the mate plant's tough seeds, which have evolved to sprout only after passing through the guts of a bird. Like many plants originating in the forests of South America (see RUBBER), yerba mate has been difficult to adapt to growth on plantations because the higher density of trees makes them more vulnerable to diseases and pests.

The Guaraní people say the plant was presented to them by the Moon Goddess as a reward after one of the elders saved her life. Because of this, it became a sacred plant to them.

The Sacred Bush

I see Piki out in the forest as the blue and the sun come through and the Goddess of the Trees watches over all. I see Piki, happy to be beside his beloved mother as he licks his fingers after the blessings of honey. And she feels proud of her son, now eighteen years old, respectful to her and a credit to the village. I see them both going down to Carapa River to fill their water jars, where the Tropical Kingbird sings from the trees and the Cinnamon Teal from the water.

And on their way, waiting in a yerba mate bush to greet them, is White Spider, Piki's childhood friend. Piki is his hero. You see, back in their formative years, Piki saved his arachnid companion from drowning, sealing their friendship forever. White Spider greets them:

WHITE SPIDER
Good Morning, Mama. Piki,
Greetings, my friend,
Wishing a good day to you both.

PIKI
Same to you, little friend.
I hope you are well—
The sun shines for you also.

While in conversation by the sacred bush, Piki sees something his eyes delight in—generating glint, giving birth to dream. And he would remember later that as she came gliding by in her canoe, the fragrance of the jasmine flowers heightened, as if heralding her presence. The one who passed by on that momentous morning was one whose name he did not know.

Piki, eager to hear, and his mother happy to tell, tells him of Tukira. Tukira, gentle and beautiful, daughter of the chief and beloved by all, especially her peers of the male persuasion. Piki joins the queue! And the initial meeting of wonderful surprise becomes a regular encounter by happy arrangement. Soon, everyone knows that they are together, that love has empowered their interaction: that the Saffron Finch sings only for them.

But you know how fathers are, rich or poor; they want the best for their "princesses." So even though he likes Piki, he sends word near and far to Tukira's hopeful suitors, giving them all a chance. And they come in droves. So the trials are set: some of skill and one of imagination. Skill trials include being the first to catch a jaguar and winning the swimming race of Carapa River. Piki wins his fair share of competitions and shines in the others, remaining at the head of the queue.

But the feat of imagination seems to ensnare him. Not that he doesn't have any—far from it. But as he is a poor man, how can he compare with the others? You see, the chief has asked the suitors to think hard and bring the greatest gift to Tukira. So there's Piki, thinking he can't compete with all the jewelry of precious gems and the tapestries of highest-grade silk being offered. It is a time to lament as he sits by a yerba mate bush:

PIKI
What shall I do, Saffron Finch?
Tell me, what shall I do?
Go to the pine tree,
And collect a little sap,
Sticking Tukira to me?
Tell me, tell me,
Shall pine sap become our glue?

And his other friend, smaller than the finch, hearing the lament of his former rescuer, answers the SOS.

WHITE SPIDER
Don't worry, my friend,
All will be well.
I am the ringer,
And I carry the bell.
I'll play a melody for you.
A Piki melody,
Sprinkled with harmony.
I am your friend in need.

Re-emphasizing that all will be well, he sends Piki home, telling him to return the next morning. And during the evening, on behalf of his human friend, he undertakes a wondrous night shift. We see a master at his trade. He weaves and weaves, and in his weaving appear the passion fruit flower, banana frond, jasmine flower, yerba mate leaf, and other flora, all presented in silk.

The anxious one, awakening, gulps down some papaya juice and rushes to the sacred bush, the residence of his oldest friend. He doesn't see the iridescence of the Vermilion Flycatcher or the colors of the Yellow Parakeet. All he sees is Tukira.

And then, seeing what else is waiting for him, a grin appears on his face for the first time in days. A grin and a jump around! He knows he's in with a winning chance now. He tickles the spider and massages all eight of his limbs, weary after the night's endeavor. Then, he places his hand across his chest, bows to his friend, and rushes off to the residence of the chief. And of all the gifts assembled before the celebrated young woman, not one compares to what his diminutive friend produced. So as destiny envisaged, Piki and Tukira are married.

Faces are painted, cassava beer is drunk, maracas are shaken, and bodies move in dance. Piki gives thanks to God, whom his people call Tupa; to his longtime friend, Little White Spider; and to the sacred bush called yerba mate. And the Ruby Hummingbird and the Amethyst Woodstar lead the village in singing.

RUBY AND AMETHYST
Karma, karma,
We sing of karma,
Of one helping the other.
Piki saved White Spider
And he returned the favor.

Yerba mate,
Yerba mate,
Piki got Tukira.

Glossary of Persons

AMADOU HAMPÂTÉ BÂ
Born in Mali, Bâ was a 20th century Fulani researcher, writer and cultural ambassador, who undertook a lot of research into Fulani orality.

BASSEKOU KOUYATE
From one of the great jali lineages, Bassekou Kouyate is a celebrated player of the ngoni, one of the traditional instruments of the Mande griot. *See* Jali.

BIRAGO DIOP
A Senegalese writer, veterinary surgeon, folklorist and diplomat who is the eponymous figure of Birago Day: African and Caribbean Folklore Day. He wrote *The Tales of Amadou Koumba*, first published in French in 1947 and in English in 1966.

GEBRE HANNA
An Ethiopian historical figure known for his wit and friendship with Emperor Menelik II. After his death, he became a central character in Amharic folklore.

KULANG TOAT
From the Nuer people of South Sudan, Kulang Toat was a controversial figure of the 20th century who went on to become a major figure in Nuer orality.

JAH FOLK
The original mouthpiece of Rootical Folklore, making his initial appearances in my digital collection *The Papine Tales* (Wisemind, 2022.) *See* p. 59.

LEONA WATSON
The iconic figure of Cariso, a traditional music of St. Croix.

LILIANE NERETTE LOUIS
Haitian storyteller, writer, leaf doctor, and cook, resident in America.

FUMU LIYONGO
Pokomo and Swahili culture hero. Historical ruler and poet, he is the eponymous hero of an East African epic.

MAMA SOLACE
Like Jah Folk, Mama Solace is a mouthpiece of Rootical Folklore. *See* p. 11

MBOMBE
In the Lianja Epic of the Mongo, Mbombe is the wrestler heroine, who marries the man who defeats her in a bout.

MENELIK II
19th /20th-century emperor of Ethiopia and founder of the capital city Addis Ababa, which means "New Flower," thus named by Menelik's wife, Empress Taytu.

MISS LOU (LOUISE BENNETT-COVERLEY)
Iconic figure in Jamaican folklore. Storyteller, poet, actor, and writer. First Black student at RADA, the Royal Academy of Dramatic Arts.

MODIBO MUHAMMED AL-KABURI
Of Fulani heritage, one of the leading academics of Timbuktu University, which had its Golden Age in the 16th century.

NANA ASMAU

Fulani poet, teacher and linguist, she was the founder of Yan Taru, an educational initiative for teenage wives, in 19th century Hausaland, northern Nigeria.

OBA ESIGIE

A 16th century ruler of the Edo people in the Kingdom of Benin, Oba [king] Esigie was supported by his mother Idia, known for her advisory, healing and martial skills. He made her the first Iyoba or Queen Mother of the Edo.

OZIDI

Eponymous hero of an epic of the Ijo/Ijaw people of Nigeria. Transcribed by poet and playwright John Pepper Clark, it was published in 1977 as the Ozidi Saga.

PURA BELPRÉ

Puerto Rican storyteller, writer and librarian, who told stories in Spanish as well as English, in the early 20th century New York library system.

SILAMAKA

A Fulani hero who favored a certain tamarind tree. A version of the Epic of Silamaka and Poullori was collected and translated by Amadou Hampâté Bâ and Lilyan Kestelot. *See* Amadou Hampâté Bâ.

SLY AND ROBBIE

One of the great drum (Sly) and bass (Robbie) partnerships of reggae music.

SUNDIATA

The eponymous hero of the Mandinka epic, founder of the 13th-century Mali Empire. The epic was first published in English in 1965.

TWINS SEVEN SEVEN

Prince Twins Seven Seven, 20th century Yoruba artist, whose work was influenced by the oral traditions.

UCHE OKEKE

Artist and educator, founder of Ulism, a form of art based on the traditional Igbo celebratory painting of bodies and walls known as Uli.

Glossary of Terms

ADIMU
Offerings of food—either cooked or as picked—for the orishas, the deities of Yoruba belief. Each orisha has flora associated with them.

ASHE
Spiritual essence, or energy. All living things posses ashe. Babalawaos and iyalawos—Yoruba priests—use the ashe of plants in their prescriptions following divination.

ANANSI
Celebrated arachnid of African and Diasporic folklore. First known among the Ashanti of Ghana, through transatlantic slavery, this trickster spider became a feature in Caribbean orality.

ASO
Also known as Crooky and Okonare Yaa, Aso is the wife of Anansi: the epitome of patience.

BABALAWO
Yoruba priest, practioner of Ifa, the Yoruba form of divination

BAMANA
The Bamana are one of the Mande peoples, found throughout West Africa. They were the founders of the Segu and Kaarta kingdoms in Mali.

BAULE

A people of the Ivory Coast, related to the Ashanti in neighbouring Ghana. Their art influenced artists such as Amedeo Modigliani. Compare Baule motifs—such as
almond eyes, elongated nose and small mouth—with Modigliani's sculpture, Head of a Woman. He would have seen Baule art in the Trocadero, alongside his friend Brancusi.

BENDRE

Sacred drum of the Mossi/Moose people of Burkina Faso. The body of the instrument is a calabash. Bendré is also the term for the player of this drum.

BOGOLANFINI

Meaning "mud with cloth," it is a form of textile, mainly associated with the Bamana/Bambara people of Mali. It is woven by men, dyed by women, and decorated with fermented mud.

CANDOMBLÉ

A religion founded in Bahia, Brazil during the transatlantic slave trade and inspired by Yoruba, Fon, Bantu, Indigenous and European influences. Umbanda, also of Brazil, was influenced by Candomblé.

CARISO

Traditional form of music and social commentary in St Croix, one of the US Virgin Islands. Sung by women, with men drumming. Leona Watson is the iconic figure of Cariso.

CHI WARA

Amongst the Bamana of Mali, Chi Wara is the trailblazing icon of agriculture, a fusion of aardvak, antelope and pangolin. In their orality, he taught them the rudiments of cultivation. The Chi Wara is depicted in sculpture as well as in masks, which are danced.

DUDU OSUN
The black soap of West Africa. Used hygenically, and as part of balalawo/ iyalawo prescriptions, after Ifa divination, in Orisha belief. *See* Orunmila.

DUPPY
Jamaican word for a ghost.

EWE
A Yoruba word for plants.

FETEFETE
In the folklore of the Mongo, of the Democratic Republic of the Congo, Fetefete is the guardian of the safu nut tree.

GEWEL
The traditional, hereditary bard of the Wolof people of Senegal and Gambia. *See* Jali.

IFA
Yoruba form of divination using sixteen cowrie shells, kola or palm nuts and facilitated by a babalawo or iyalawo. Orunmila is the orisha of Yoruba divination.

IFE
Spiritual heartland of the Yoruba, where they believe humanity began. Major events, such as the Olojo Festival in honor of Ogun, are held there. *See* Ogun.

IYALAWO / IYANIFA
Female priest of Orisha belief. Her male counterpart is

the babalawo.

IYEROSUN
Sacred dust, generated by termites from the Camwood tree and used in Ifa divination.

KORA
One of the three main instruments, along with the ngoni and the balafon, associated with the jali of the Mande peoples. A lute of twenty-one strings, formerly made of animal skin, now of fishing line. *See* Jali.

LOA / LWA
Loa or lwa are the spirits of Vodun, the national belief of Benin, and its Haitian derivative, Vodou.

LUKUMÍ / SANTERÍA / REGLA DE OCHA
Founded in Cuba, this is one of the diasporic religions, derived from Yoruba religion with Catholic influences. It centers around worship of the orishas.

LUSCA
Resident in the blue holes, he's an aquatic ogre of Bahamian folklore, a fusion of shark and octopus.

MOSSI/MOOSE
The most populous of the peoples of Burkina Faso and founders of a medieval state.

NOMKHUBLWANE
Zulu female deity of rain and the natural world, connected to the earth and fertility.

NUER
The Nuer are one of the Nilotic peoples, a group which includes the more well known Maasai. They are pastoralists, living a life in which cattle are

paramount.

OONI
Title of the ruler of Ife, the Yoruba spiritual heartland.

PAPA BWA
He's the guardian of the forest in Trinidadian and St.Lucian folklore.

PAPA LEGBA
In Vodou, he is the loa (spirit) of the gateway, roads and messages. His Orisha counterpart is Eshu, known also as Eleuga and Exu.

SANTERÍA
See Lukumí

SASABONSAM
The ogre of Ashanti folklore, resident of trees, from where he generates entrapment.

SHETANI
The malevolent spirits of Swahili folklore. Shulewele is also a shetani, but less of the demonic strain runs through him: he's a collector of plants for medicine.

SONNINKE
A people dwelling in the borderland region of Mauritania and Senegal. From their culture comes the *Dausi* epic, which features Samba Gana—for me, one of the great heroes of West African folklore.

SOUCOUYANT
An ordinary citizen by day; at night, she sheds her skin, transforming into a fireball witch, emblazoning the sky.

TERRIEROS

Temples of the followers of Candomblé and Umbanda in Brazil.

UMBANDA

One of the Afro-Brazilian religions of the Diaspora. Influenced by Candomblé, but more urban, founded in Rio de Janeiro in the 1920s. Quimbanda, a related tradition, lacks Umbanda's Catholic influences and has sometimes been pejoratively characterized as "black magic." *See* Candomblé

VODOU

The Haitian derivative of Vodun, the national belief of Benin.

YAN DAWA

The little protectors of the forest, in the orality of the Hausa of northern Nigeria.

ZARMA

A people of Niger with a strong connection to the Songhai, who ruled Mali during the Golden Age of Timbuktu University.

Glossary of Orishas

The orishas (also orisas, orichas, orixás) are divinities in the religion of the Yoruba-speaking peoples of West Africa and in the many religious traditions that derive from it throughout the African Diaspora. Within these traditions, there is much variation. This glossary is not a definitive guide but is intended to provide some additional context for the pieces in this book. A few introductory resources (all of an academic bent) on the topic of orisha religions include:

Fernández Olmos, Margarite and Lizabeth Paravisini-Gebert, eds. 2022. *Creole Religions of the Caribbean: An Introduction: From Vodou and Santería to Obeah and Espiritismo.* 3rd edition. Religion, Race, and Ethnicity. New York: NYU Press.

Olupona, Jacob K. 2008. *Òrìṣà Devotion as World Religion: The Globalization of Yorùbá Religious Culture.* Madison: The University of Wisconsin Press.

Parés, Luis Nicolau. 2013. *The Formation of Candomblé: Vodun History and Ritual in Brazil.* Durham, NC: UNC Press Books.

AGANJU

Orisha of the wilderness and deserts. He has a strong connection to Shango, orisha of thunder and lightning. Like some other orishas, he's said to have been a historical figure, later deified. Like Shango, he was associated with the Oyo State. *Associated plants:* dates

BABALÚ-AYÉ

Babalú-Ayé is the orisha of disease and healing. In Lukumí, an African diasporic religion of Cuba, he is associated with St. Lazarus, patron saint of the sick and poor. In Rincón, Cuba, there is a leprosarium and a church dedicated to him, where many Cubans make a pilgrimage on his saint day of December 17th. *Associated plants*: chili pepper, peanut, sarsaparilla, soursop, tamarind

ESHU

Orisha of the gateway, roads, and messages which go between Olodumore (Supreme Being), his orishas, and us. Known as Elegua amongst the Santería creyentes (believers) in Cuba and as Exu to the followers of Candomblé and Umbanda in Brazil. *Associated plants*: bamboo, cassava, chili pepper, guava, mallow, pea, raspberry, sugarcane, tobacco, yam

IBEJI

Eponymous orisha from the Yoruba word for "twins," of which the Yoruba produce a very high number. Prince Twins Seven Seven was the one surviving member of seven sets of twins. *Associated plants*: arrowroot, mango, soursop

OBA

Orisha of the eponymous Oba River. In the patakis (ancient stories), she has a rivalry with Oshun. Said to have been a daughter of Yemoja. *Associated plants*: cherry

OBATALA

Orisha of human creation; some say of Earth's creation also, but other versions say it was Oduduwa. He is seen as a father figure, benevolent to all, especially those in less-abled bodies. Known as Oxala in Candomblé and Umbanda. *Associated plants*: acacia, basil, breadfruit, shea

OCHOSI

Associated with forests and hunting as well as with justice. He has a close association with Ogun, orisha of iron: Ogun clears the forest with his machete so Ochosi can hunt with bow and arrows. Known in Candomblé and Ubanda as Oxossi. *Associated plants*: pea

ODUDUWA

Orisha of Earth's Creation, although some versions say the task was facilitated by Obatala. He has a foundational connection to Ife, the heartland city of Yoruba spirituality. *Associated plants*: yam

OGUN

Orisha representing iron. One of the major deities, because iron permeates all our lives; hairdresser, mechanic, farmer, taxi driver, pilot, blacksmith and so on. Known as Ogun Feraille in Vodou (Haiti) and Oggun in Lukumí (Cuba). *Associated plants*: alfalfa, alligator pepper, bamboo, cassava, eucalyptus, kapok, mango, palm

OKO

Known as Oco in Candomblé, he is the orisha of farms and agriculture. The casing of his ritual staff, also called a sword, is made from fabric, embellished with beads and leather. *Associated plants*: kapok, soursop, sweet potato, yam

OLODUMORE

Also known as Olorun, he is the Supreme Being of Orisha belief. He cannot be influenced or appeased, so there are no shrines, designated days, or offerings to him.

OLOKUN

Orisha of the sea and wealth, variously presented as male, female, or nonbinary depending on the tradition. Their name is a contraction of the Yoruba "Olo Okun" meaning "owner of the ocean." The Edo people, neighbors of the Yoruba, see the crocodile as the messenger of Olokun. *Associated plants*: balsam apple

ORI

Orisha of our spiritual essence. Ori means "head," the interior of which is the place of thought and reflection, our stepping-stones to a higher consciousness.

ORUNMILA

Associated with wisdom and Ifa. Ifa is the Yoruba form of divination, using cowrie shells, kola or palm nuts, sixteen in number. Babalawos and Iyalawos—male and female priests, practitioners of Ifa—have a deep connection to this orisha. Known as Orula or Orunla in Lukumí.

OSANYIN

Orisha of plants and healing. Thought of and depicted as disfigured, with only one eye, arm and leg. Alongside Orunmila, he is paramount to Yoruba priests, as plants are a major part of their prescriptions, following divination. Known as Ossaim in Candomblé and Umbanda. *Associated plants*: works with all plants; especially linked with healing herbs such as bay geranium or rue.

OSHUN (OSUN)

An orisha of rivers and love; Oya, Oba and Yemoja, also female, are other river deities. She is known as

Oxum in Candomblé and Ubanda and Ochun in Lukumí. *Associated plants*: african lettuce, chamomile, grapefruit, orange, rosemary, vanilla, water cabbage

OYA

She is the orisha of wind and storms, known as a protector of women. She is also the deity of the River Niger, one of the great thoroughfares of West Africa, past and present. Also known as Iansã. *Associated plants*: cloves, eggplant, flame tree, onion, papaya

SHANGO

Orisha of thunder and lighning. His symbol is a double-headed axe. Like Ochosi, he is associated with justice. Known as Chango in Lukumí, Ogou Chango in Vodou and Xango in Candomblé and Umbanda. *Associated plants*: calabash, chili pepper, fig, flame tree, flame vine, okra, plantain

YEMOJA

Orisha of otherhood, seas and rivers. In Nigeria, this orisha is the patron deity of Ibadan and in Brazil, an annual festival takes place on Salvador beach, in Bahia. Also known as Lemanja, Yemanja, Yemaya, and other similar variants. *Associated plants*: aloe, geranium, papaya, rose, watermelon

Index of Species

Scientific	English	Yoruba / Lukumí	Spanish	Portuguese	French	p.
Adansonia digitata	baobab	igi ose	baobab	baobá	baobab	28
Aframomum danielii or melegueta	alligator pepper, grains of paradise	ataare	amomo	pimenta-da-costa, malagueta	maniguette, poivre de Guinée	12
Allium spp.	onion	alubosa	cebolla	cebola	oignon	156
Aloe vera syn. barbadensis	aloe	ahon erin	sábila	babosa	aloès, laloi	16
Ambrosia hispida	bay geranium, coastal ragweed	~ / mireure	carquesa, altamisa de playa	~	set vil, tapis	94
Ananas comosus	pineapple	ope oyinbo	piña	abacaxi[2]	ananas[2]	180
Annona muricata	soursop	eko oyinbo / nichularafún	guanábana[2]	graviola	corossolier	218
Arachis hypogaea	peanut, goober nut[1]	epa	maní[2]	amendoim[2]	cacahouète[2], pistache [de terre]	170

Scientific	English	Yba / Lkm	Spanish	Portuguese	French	P.
Artocarpus altilis	breadfruit	berefurutu pan	árbol del pan	árvore-do-pão	arbre à pain, châtaigni-er-pays	46
Blighia sapida	ackee[1]	isin	seso vegetal	morentina, castanheiro-de-áfrica	aki[1]	4
Bougainvillea spp.	bougainvillea	ˋ	bugambilia	primavera, três-marias	bougainvillier	44
Capsicum spp.	chili pepper[2]	ata ijosi / kayuedin	ají[2]	pimentão, pimen-ta-malagueta	piment	65
Carica papaya	papaya[2]	ibepe	fruta bomba	mamão, ababaia[2]	papaye[2]	164
Ceiba pentandra	kapok	araba / iroko	ceiba[2]	mafumeira[2]	mapou[2], fromager	123
Chrysophyllum cainito	star-apple, golden leaf tree	osan agbalumo (*Gameya spp.*) / asán	caimito[2]	caimito[2]	caimite[2]	222
Citrullus lanatus	watermelon	egusi baara / abeye	sandía	melancia	pastèque, melon d'eau	258

Scientific	English	Yba / Lkm	Spanish	Portuguese	French	p.
Citrus × limon	lemon	orombo	limón	limão-siciliano	limon [France]	129
Citrus × paradisi	grapefruit	′	toronja	pomelo	chadèque (C. maxima)	98
Citrus × aurantium	orange	osan / orombo	naranja	laran- ja(-da-terra)	orange douce	159
Cocos nucifera	coconut palm	agbon / obi	coco	coqueiro	cocotier	70
Cola acuminata	kola[1] tree	obi	nuez de cola[1]	ervilha-de- pombo, jero	cola[1] mâle	12
Colocasia esculenta	taro, dasheen	koko pupa	malanga[1] (isleña)	inhame[1]	caraïbe, malanga deux palles[1]	238
Crescentia cujete	calabash (tree)	′ / egwa, igba	güira	cuitê[2]	calebasse marron	50
Cucumis sativus	cucumber	apala	pepino	pepino	concombre	72
Cucumis anguria	maroon cucumber	′	pepinillo, pepino del monte	maxixe[2]	ti-concombre	72
Curcubita spp.	pumpkin, squash	elegede	calabaza	abóbora, jerimum[2]	giraumon[2]	186

Scientific	English	Yba / Lkm	Spanish	Portuguese	French	P.
Cymbopogon citratus	lemongrass	koriko oba	limoncillo, caña santa	capim-santo	citronelle	133
Dacryodes edulis	butterfruit	elemi	✓	✓	safou	208
Delonix regia	flame tree	ogun bereke, sekeseke / igi tambina, inaweko	framboyán	flamboiã	flamboyant	90
Diospyros mespiliformis	jackalberry, African ebony	igi dudu	✓	✓	kaki de brousse, ébène africain	116
Dioscorea spp.	yam[1]	isu, esuru / ichu, osura	ñame[1]	inhame[1]	igname[1]	260
Elaeis guineensis	African oil palm	ope eyin	palma (de aceite) africana	palmeira-de-dendê[1]	palme à huile	162
Encephalartos natalensis	Natal cycad	✓	✓	✓	✓	148
Eucalyptus globulus	eucalyptus	✓	eucalipto	eucalipto	gommier bleu	84
Ficus spp. (*gomelleira, calyptroceras et al.*)	strangler fig, banyan	[ojé] renaco		gameleira-branca, iroko		114

Scientific	English	Yba / Lkm	Spanish	Portuguese	French	p.
Ficus thonningii, natalensis, burkei	strangler fig	odan	˅	˅	˅	86
Fragaria × ananassa	strawberry	˅	fresa	morango	fraise	226
Heliconia spp.	lobster claw		bijao, platanillo	caeté, bananeira do mato	z'yeux à crabe, petit balisier	104
Hevea brasiliensis	Pará rubber tree	˅	árbol del caucho[2]	seringueira	arbre à caoutchouc[2]	202
Hibiscus sabdariffa	sorrel, roselle	isapa	(flor de) jamaica	caruru-azedo	oseille de Guinée	108
Hymenaea courbaril	West Indian locust, stinking toe	guapinol	jatobá[2], jutaí[2]	courbaril		120
Ilex paraguariensis	yerba mate	˅	yerba mate	erva-mate	yerba mate	262
Ipomoea batatas	sweet potato	kukundunku	papa dulce[2]	batata-doce[2], jetica[2]	patate[2]	232
Lagenaria siceraria	calabash, bottle gourd	igba	bangaña	cabaça	calebasse courant	50
Launaea taraxacifolia	african lettuce	yanrin	˅	˅	˅	6

Scientific	English	Yba / Lkm	Spanish	Portuguese	French	P.
Malachra capitata	Brazil jute, horse mallow	malva-de-caballo				139
Mangifera indica	mango	mongoro / oro, eleso	mango	manga	mangue	142
Manihot esculenta	cassava	ege funfun, kpaki, gbaguda	yuca	mandioca	manioc	53
Maranta arundinacea	arrowroot[2]	`	sagu, arrurruz[2]	araruta[2], embiri[2]	dictame	18
Matricaria reticuta	chamomile	`	manzanilla	camomila	camomille	56
Medicago sativa	alfalfa, lucerne	`	mielga	alfalfa	luzerne	8
Milicia excelsa	African teak	iroko	`	`	`	114
Momordica balsamina	balsam apple, cerasee	ejinrin (igbo)	balsamina, cundeamor de Cuba	`	courgette africaine, assorossi	22
Momordica charantia	bitter gourd, cerasee	ejinrin (wewe)	ampalea, cundeamor chino, caigua amarga	melão-de-São-Caetano	margose, concombre amer, pom-me-coolie, yesquin	22

290

Scientific	English	Yba / Lkm	Spanish	Portuguese	French	p.
Musa x ssp.	banana[1]	ogede	plátano (guineo)	banana[1], pacova[2]	banane[1], figue	26
Musa x ssp.	plantain	agbagba / ogede	plátano	banana-da-terra[1]	banane plantain	182
Myristica fragrans	nutmeg	´	nuez moscada	noz-moscada	(noix de) muscade	150
Nicotiana tabacum	tobacco	taba	tabaco	fumo	tabac	241
Nymphaea nouchali var. caerulea	blue lotus	´	´	nenúfar azul		39
Ocimum basilicum	basil	akeroro, efinrin wewe / ororo	albahaca	manjericão, alfavaca	basilic	36
Oxytenanthera abyss-inica	savannah bamboo	apako, (o) parun (pupa) / paki (for B. vulgaris)	´	´	bambou	24
Pennisetum glaucum	millet	emeye	mijo	milho, milheto	ti-mil chandelle	145
Persea americana	avocado	pia nla / itobi, akatara	aguacate[2]	abacate[2]	avocat[2]	20

Scientific	English	Yba / Lkm	Spanish	Portuguese	French	P.
Phoenix dactylifera	date palm	okunkun (related species)	datilero, támara	tamareira	dattier	78
Pinus caribaea	Caribbean pine	okilan, orukonyikan, yemao	pino macho	ˇ	pin caraïbe	177
Pistia stratiotes	water lettuce	oju oro	lechuguilla	repolho d'água, mururé-pagé[2]	salade d'eau	254
Prunus serotina var. *salicifolia*	wild black cherry	ˇ	capulín[2]	ˇ	ˇ	62
Psidium guajava	guava[2]	goroba[2]	guayaba[2]	(araçá-)goiaba[2]	gouyave[2]	100
Pyrostegia venusta	flame vine	ˇ	liana de fuego, tango	cipó-de-são-joão	liane aurore	92
Pyrus spp.	pear	ˇ	pera	pera	poire	173
Rhamnus prinoides	shiny-leaf buckthorn					96
Rosa spp.	rose	ˇ / idon, dido	rosa	rosa	rose	193
Rubus idaeus	raspberry	ˇ	frambuesa	framboesa	framboise	190

Scientific	English	Yba / Lkm	Spanish	Portuguese	French	p.
Ruta graveolens, chalepensis	rue	atopa kun	ruda	arruda	rue, citronelle marron	205
Saccharum officinarum	sugarcane	ireke	caña (de azucar)	cana-de-açúcar	canne à sucre	230
Salvia rosmarinus	rosemary	⌐ / ewe re	romero	alecrim	romarin	200
Senecio rhyncholaenus	[ibhulu]	⌐	⌐	⌐	⌐	112
Smilax balbisiana	chaney root	ka(n)san (S. anceps) / atewe edin (S. havanensis)	⌐	⌐	⌐	60
Smilax ornata syn. S. regelii	sarsaparilla	⌐	zarzaparrilla	salsepareille	⌐	212
Solanum aethiopicum	garden egg	ikan	berenjena escarlata	jiló[1]	gilo[1]	82
Sorghum bicolor	sorghum	oka baba / okableba	milo, mijo grande	sorgo, milho-zaburro	sorgho	216
Syzygium aromaticum syn. Caryophyllus aromaticus	cloves	⌐	palo clavo	cravo-da-índia	girofle	68
Syzygium jambos	rose-apple	/ yilebo, echikacho	pomarrosa	jambo branco	jamrosat	196

Scientific	English	Yba / Lkm	Spanish	Portuguese	French	p.
Tamarindus indica	tamarind	ajagbon / igi iyagbon	tamarindo	tamarindo, jubaí[2]	tamarinier	234
Taxodium mucronatum	Montezuma cypress	✓	ahuehuete[2]	✓	✓	76
Tecoma stans	yellow cedar	✓	tronadora	ipê-de-jardim	chevalier	245
Vachellia nilotica syn. *Acacia nilotica*	gum arabic acacia	ewon	✓	✓	gommier rouge, gonakié[1]	1
Vanilla planifolia	vanilla	✓	vainilla	baunilha	vanille	250
Vigna unguiculata	cowpea, black-eyed pea	eree ahun / guendi	frijol carita	feijão-frade	niébé[1]	166
Vitellaria paradoxa	shea[1]	emi gidi	karité[1]	carité	karité	214

[1] denotes a word in a European language that derives from an African language [2] denotes a word in a European language that derives from an Indigenous American language

Some sources for the common names given in this index include Ajao (2022), Cabrera (2023), Verger (1995), and Voeks (1997). See "Further Reading: Ethnobotanical Bibliography" for these and other references.

Further Reading

FOLKLORE COLLECTIONS

Abrahams, Roger. 1999. *African American Folktales: Stories from Black Traditions in the New World*. New York: Pantheon.

Anthony, Michael. 2005. *Caribbean Folk Tales & Fantasies*. Oxford: MacMillan Caribbean.

Bacha, Mohamed. 2015. *Tunisian Folktales: Five Stories From The Oral Storytelling Tradition*. Self-published.

Barlow, Genevieve. 1966. *Latin American Tales: From the Pampas to the Pyramids of Mexico*. Chicago: Rand McNally.

Baumann, Margaret. 1929. *Ajapa the Tortoise: A Book of Nigerian Folk Tales*. London: A.C. Black.

Belcher, Stephen. 2005. *African Myths of Origin*. Penguin Classics. London: Penguin Random House.

Belpré, Pura. 1965. *The Tiger and the Rabbit and Other Tales*. Philadelphia: J. B. Lippincott Company.

———. 1973. *Once in Puerto Rico*. New York: Warne.

Bennett, Louise. 1979. *Anancy and Miss Lou*. Kingston: Sangster's Book Stores.

Berry, Jack. 1991. *West African Folktales*. Edited by Richard Spears. Chicago: Northwestern University Press.

Brailsford, David. 2001. *Duppy Stories*. Kingston: LMH Publishing Company.

Burke, Eddie. 1975. *Water in the Gourd, and Other Jamaican Folk Stories*. London: Oxford University Press.

Cancel, Robert. 2015. *Storytelling in Northern Zambia : Theory, Method, Practice and Other Necessary Fictions*. Cambridge: Open Book Publishers.

Clark-Bekederemo, J. P. 1991. *The Ozidi Saga*. Washington, D.C: Howard University Press.

Courlander, Harold. 1968. *The Piece of Fire: And Other Haitian Tales*.

New York: Harcourt, Brace & World.

———. 1976. *A Treasury of African Folklore: The Oral Literature, Traditions, Myths, Legends, Epics, Tales, Recollections, Wisdom, Sayings, and Humor of Africa.* New York: Crown.

Cushman, Amanda. 2010. *Zarma Folktales of Niger.* Williamsburg, MA: Quale Press.

de Almeida, Livia, and Ana Maria Portella. 2006. *Brazilian Folktales.* Exeter: Libraries Unlimited.

Denham, Bish. 2014. *Anansi and Company: Retold Jamaican Tales.* Kerrville, TX: Bound Post.

DeSpain, Pleasant. 2005. *Eleven Turtle Tales.* Little Rock, AR: August House.

Egudu, Romanus. 1973. *The Calabash of Wisdom and Other Igbo Stories.* New York: NOK.

Elliot, Geraldine. 1949. *Where the Leopard Passes: A Book of African Folktales.* London: Routledge & Kegan Paul.

Elswit, Sharon Barcan. 2015. *The Latin American Story Finder: A Guide to 470 Tales from Mexico, Central America and South America, Listing Subjects and Sources.* Jefferson, NC: McFarland.

———. 2017. *The Caribbean Story Finder: A Guide to 438 Tales from 24 Nations and Territories, Listing Subjects and Sources.* Jefferson, NC: McFarland.

Laird, Elizabeth and Michael Sargent. n.d. *Ethiopian Folktales: The Story Collecting Project.* https://www.ethiopianfolktales.com/en/the-project.

Hazelton, Hugh, Patricia Aldana, and Luis Garay. 1996. *Jade and Iron: Latin American Tales from Two Cultures.* Toronto: Douglas & McIntyre.

Ishmael, Odeen. 2011. *Guyana Legends: Folk Tales of the Indigenous Amerindians.* Self-published.

Johnson, John William, Thomas A. Hale, and Stephen Paterson Belcher. 1997. *Oral Epics from Africa: Vibrant Voices from a Vast Continent.* Bloomington: Indiana University Press.

Johnston, H. A. S. 1966. *A Selection of Hausa Stories.* London: Clarendon Press.

Magel, Emil A. 1984. *Folktales from the Gambia: Wolof Fictional Narratives.* Washington, D.C: Lynne Rienner.

Mama, Raouf, ed. 1998. *Why Goats Smell Bad and Other Stories from Benin.* North Haven, CT: Linnet Books.

Mbitu, Ngangar, and Ranchor Prime. 1997. *Essential African Mythology.* London: Thorsons.

Ottley, Carlton R. 1962. *Legends: True Stories and Old Sayings from Trinidad and Tobago.* Publisher unknown.

Owomoyela, Oyekan. 1997. *Yoruba Trickster Tales.* Lincoln, NE: University of Nebraska Press.

Sánchez-González, Lisa. 2014. *Puerto Rican Folktales / Cuentos folclóricos puertorriqueños.* New York: 2Leaf Press.

Shearer, Wendy. 2021. *African and Caribbean Folktales, Myths and Legends.* London: Scholastic UK.

Sherlock, Philip M. 1956. *Anansi, the Spider Man: Jamaican Folk Tales.* London: MacMillan & Co.

Sissao, Alain-Joseph. 2010. *Folktales from the Moose of Burkina Faso.* Cameroon: Langaa.

Strong, Polly. 1992. *African Tales: Folklore of the Central African Republic.* Mogadore, OH: Telcraft.

ETHNOBOTANICAL BIBLIOGRAPHY

Adéwálé, Ifábùkúnmi O. 2021. *Àkòsé: Extraordinary Plants: Their Medicinal and Spiritual Attributes.* N.p. Adewura Natural Remedies, LLC.

Ajao, Abdulwakeel A., Yusuf Ola Mukaila, and Saheed Sabiu. 2022. "Wandering through Southwestern Nigeria: An Inventory of Yoruba Useful Angiosperm Plants." *Heliyon* 8 (1): e08668.

Cabrera, Lydia. 2023. *El Monte: Notes on the Religions, Magic, and Folklore of the Black and Creole People of Cuba.* Translated by David Font-Navarrete. Durham, NC: Duke University Press.

Carney, Judith A., and Richard N. Rosomoff. 2009. *In the Shadow of Slavery: Africa's Botanical Legacy in the Atlantic World.* Berkeley, CA: University of California Press.

National Research Council. 1996-2008. *Lost Crops of Africa.* 3 vols. Washington, D.C: The National Academies Press.

Ogunbemi, Maria. 2015. *Ritual Use of Plants in Lucumí Tradition,* 3rd Edition. Self-published.

Opie, Frederick D. 2015. *Zora Neale Hurston on Florida Food: Recipes, Remedies & Simple Pleasures.* Charleston, SC: The History Press.

Penniman, Leah. 2018. *Farming While Black: Soul Fire Farm's Practical Guide to Liberation on the Land.* White River Junction, VT: Chelsea Green Publishing.

Sokoh, Ozoz. 2017. *Kitchen Butterfly: Exploring and mapping intersec-*

tions between Nigerian cuisine and foods of the world (blog.) https://www.kitchenbutterfly.com/.

Swiecicki, Atava Garcia. 2022. *The Curanderx Toolkit: Reclaiming Ancestral Latinx Plant Medicine and Rituals for Healing.* Berkeley, CA: Heyday.

Verger, Pierre. 1995. *Ewé : The Use of Plants in Yoruba Society.* São Paulo: Editora Schwarcz.

Voeks, Robert A. 1997. *Sacred Leaves of Candomblé: African Magic, Medicine, and Religion in Brazil.* Austin: University of Texas Press.

———. 2018. *The Ethnobotany of Eden: Rethinking the Jungle Medicine Narrative.* University of Chicago Press.

Voeks, Robert A., and John Rashford, eds. 2012. *African Ethnobotany in the Americas.* New York: Springer.

Zukulu, Sinegugu, Tony Dold, Tony Abbott, et al. 2012. *Medicinal and Charm Plants of Pondoland.* Gauteng: South African National Biodiversity Institute.

FOR SPECIFIC PLANTS

Acacia

David, Arlette. 2014. "Hoopoes and Acacias: Decoding an Ancient Egyptian Funerary Scene." *Journal of Near Eastern Studies* 73 (2): 235-52.

Freudenberger, Mark. 1992. "The Great Gum Gamble: A Planning Perspective on Environmental Change in Northern Senegal." Ph.D. thesis, UCLA.

Knappert, Jan. 1991. "Nature's Cures: The Swahili Tradition." *Kenya Past and Present* 23 (1): 40-46.

Ackee

Rashford, John. 2001. "Those That Do Not Smile Will Kill Me: The Ethnobotany of the Ackee in Jamaica." *Economic Botany* 55 (2): 190-211.

African Lettuce

Shackleton, C. M., M. Pasquini, and Axel W. Drescher, eds. 2009. *African Indigenous Vegetables in Urban Agriculture.* Sterling, VA: Earthscan.

Alfalfa

Carver, George Washington. 1915. "Alfalfa: The King of All Fodder Plants, Successfully Grown in Macon County, Ala." *Tuskegee Institute Agricultural Experiment Station Bulletin* no. 29.

Alligator Pepper

Osseo-Asare, Abena. 2014. *Bitter Roots: The Search for Healing Plants in Africa*. Chicago: University of Chicago Press.

Vossen, Tessa, Alexandra Towns, Sofie Ruysschaert, Diana Quiroz, and Tinde van Andel. 2014. "Consequences of the Trans-Atlantic Slave Trade on Medicinal Plant Selection: Plant Use for Cultural Bound Syndromes Affecting Children in Suriname and Western Africa." *PLOS ONE* 9 (11).

Arrowroot

Keegan, Bill and Betsy Carlson. 2004. "Talking Taíno: Eat Roots and Leave." *Times of the Islands*, Winter 2004/2005.

Balsam Apple

Griffith, Lawrence D. 2008. *Flowers and Herbs of Early America*. New Haven: Yale University Press.

McMillan, Patrick D., and A. H. Blackwell. 2013. "The Vascular Plants Collected by Mark Catesby in South Carolina: Combining the Sloane and Oxford Herbaria." *Phytoneuron* 73: 1–32.

Bamboo

Honfo, Hermann, Frédéric Chenangnon Tovissodé, Césaire Gnanglè, Sylvanus Mensah, et al. 2015. "Traditional Knowledge and Use Value of Bamboo in Southeastern Benin: Implications for Sustainable Management." *Ethnobotany Research and Applications* 14 (March): 139–53.

Rashford, John. 1995. "The Past and Present Uses of Bamboo in Jamaica." *Economic Botany* 49 (4): 395–405.

Banana

Hemp, Andreas. 2006. "The Banana Forests of Kilimanjaro: Biodiversity and Conservation of the Chagga Homegardens." *Biodiversity & Conservation* 15 (4): 1193–1217.

Kamanzi, Adalbertus. 2012. "'They Needed an Ethnographer: That Is Why They Missed It!' Exploring the Value of Bananas among the Haya People of Bukoba, Northwestern Tanzania." ASC

Working Paper Series no. 104.

Baobab

National Research Council. 1996-2008. *Lost Crops of Africa*. Vols 2 & 3. Washington, D.C: The National Academies Press.

Rashford, John. 2018. "Human Beings, Baobabs, and Tamarinds: An Evolutionary Complex." February 18, 2022. New York Botanical Garden. https://www.nybg.org/event/human-beings-bao-babs-and-tamarinds-an-evolutionary-complex/.

Basil

de Albuquerque, Ulysses P., and L.H.C. Andrade. 1998. "Etnobotánica del género *Ocimum* L.(Lamiaceae) en las comu-nidades Afrobrasileñas." In *Anales del jardín botánico de Madrid*, 56:107-18. (Spanish)

Ayre, Sylvester. 2002. *Bush Doctor: Forgotten Folklore and Remedies from the Caribbean*. Kingston: LMH.

Blue Lotus

Green, Roger L. and Michael Rosen. 2011. *Tales of Ancient Egypt*. London: Puffin. Hepper, F. N. 1990. *Pharaoh's Flowers: The Botanical Treasures of Tutankhamun*. London: HMSO.

Breadfruit

DeLoughrey, Elizabeth. 2007. "Globalizing the Routes of Breadfruit and Other Bounties." *Journal of Colonialism and Colonial History* 8 (3).

Calabash

Daybo. 2019. "The Calabash, a Cultural and Cosmological Constant." 2019. *Cultures of West Africa* (blog). June 17, 2019. https://web.archive.org/web/20221101000000*/https://www.culturesofwestafrica.com/calabash-cultural-cosmological-con-stant/

Cassava

Emery, Christina, Rachel Hirsch, and Melinda Susanto. 2022. "Cassava: From Toxic Tuber to Food Staple." *Dumbarton Oaks Plant Humanities Lab*. https://lab.plant-humanities.org/cassava/.

Chaney Root

Vandebroek, Ina, David Picking, Jessica Tretina, Jason West, et al. 2021. "Root Tonics and Resilience: Building Strength, Health, and Heritage in Jamaica." *Frontiers in Sustainable Food Systems* 5.

Cherry

Altieri, Miguel A., and Javier Trujillo. 1987. "The Agroecology of Corn Production in Tlaxcala, Mexico." *Human Ecology* 15 (2): 189–220.

Popenoe, Wilson, and Abelardo Pachano. 1922. "The Capulín Cherry: A Superior Form of the Northern Black Cherry Developed in the Highlands of Tropical America." *Journal of Heredity* 13 (2): 51–62.

Chili Pepper

Antolini, Tina. The Resurrection of the Fish Pepper: Interview with Michael Twitty, William Woys Weaver, Denzel Mitchell, and Spike Gjerde. *Okracast: The Podcast of the Southern Foodways Alliance.* Podcast audio. July 10, 2014.

Johnson-Roehr, S. N. 2022. "Plant of the Month: Chili Pepper." *JSTOR Daily.* November 3, 2022. https://daily.jstor.org/plant-of-the-month-chili-pepper/.

Cloves

Ghosh, Amitav. 2021. *The Nutmeg's Curse: Parables for a Planet in Crisis.* Chicago: University of Chicago Press.

Coconut

Lele, Ócha'ni. 2001. *Obí: Oracle of Cuban Santería.* Rochester, VT: Destiny Books.

Wood, Funlayo E. 2017. "Objects and Immortals: The Life of Obi in Ifa-Orisa Religion." PhD Thesis, Harvard University.

Cucumber

Maroyi, Alfred, 2013. "Use of Weeds as Traditional Vegetables in Shurugwi District, Zimbabwe." *Journal of Ethnobiology and Ethnomedicine* 9 (1): 1–10.

Muthukumaran, Sureshkumar. 2023. The Tropical Turn: Agricultural Innovation in the Ancient Middle East and the Mediterranean. Berkeley: University of California Press.

Paris, Harry S. 2016. "Overview of the Origins and History of the Five Major Cucurbit Crops: Issues for Ancient DNA Analysis of Archaeological Specimens." *Vegetation History and Archaeobotany*

25 (4): 405–14.

Cypress

Bowles, David. 2018. *Feathered Serpent, Dark Heart of Sky: Myths of Mexico*. El Paso: Cinco Puntos Press.

Dates

Baluang, Weirial Puok. 2019. *The Stories of Kulang Toat: A Legend in Africa's Nuer Land*. Osborne Park, W. Australia: Africa World Books.

Eggplant

National Research Council. 2006. *Lost Crops of Africa,,* Vol. 2. Washington, D.C: The National Academies Press.

Eucalyptus

Pankhurst, Richard. 1995. "The History of Deforestation and Afforestation in Ethiopia Prior to World War I." *Northeast African Studies* 2 (1): 119–33.

Fig

Janzen, Daniel H. 1979. "How to Be a Fig." *Annual Review of Ecology and Systematics* 10 (1): 13–51.

Karangi, Matthew M. 2008. "Revisiting the Roots of Gĩkũyũ Culture through the Sacred Mũgumo Tree." *Journal of African Cultural Studies* 20 (1): 117–32.

Flame Tree

Tarter, Andrew. 2015. "Trees in Vodou: An Arbori-Cultural Exploration." Journal for the Study of *Religion, Nature and Culture* 9 (April): 87–112.

Geranium

Halberstein, Robert A., and Ashley B. Saunders. 1978. "Traditional Medical Practices and Medicinal Plant Usage on a Bahamian Island." *Culture, Medicine and Psychiatry* 2 (2): 177–203.

Gesho

Gebremeskel, Destaalem, Emiru Birhane, Meley Mekonen Rannestad, Semae Gebre, and Girmay Tesfay. 2021. "Biomass and Soil Carbon Stocks of *Rhamnus Prinoides* Based Agroforestry Practice with Varied Density in the Drylands of Northern

Ethiopia." *Agroforestry Systems* 95 (7): 1275-93.

Grapefruit

Nosowitz, Dan. 2020. "Grapefruit Is One of the Weirdest Fruits on the Planet." *Atlas Obscura.* October 6, 2020. https://www.atlasobscura.com/articles/grapefruit-history-and-drug-interactions.

Smith, Frederick H., and Hayden F. Bassett. 2016. "The Role of Caves and Gullies in Escape, Mobility, and the Creation of Community Networks among Enslaved Peoples of Barbados." In Archaeologies of Slavery and Freedom in the Caribbean: Exploring the Spaces in Between, edited by Lynsey Bates, John M. Chenoweth, and James A. Delle. Gainsville: University Press of Florida.

Guava

Brown, David H. 1993. "Thrones of the Orichas: Afro-Cuban Altars in New Jersey, New York, and Havana." *African Arts* 26 (4): 44-87.

Ortega, Racso Fernández, and Juan Cuza Huart. 2010. "Opiyelguobirán y Maquetaurie Guayaba: Nueva Propuesta de Interpretación." *Cuba Arqueológica* 3 (2): 2. (Spanish)

Heliconia

Kress, W. John and Yota Batsaki. 2022. "Heliconia: Evolution at Work." *Dumbarton Oaks Plant Humanities Lab.* https://lab.plant-humanities.org/heliconia/.

Hibiscus

"The Story Behind Red-Hued Juneteenth Food and Drink." Gastro Obscura. n.d. Accessed October 28, 2023. https://www.atlasobscura.com/articles/what-is-juneteenth.

Solórzano, Andrés Triana. 2023. "Plant of the Month: Hibiscus." *JSTOR Daily* April 28, 2023. https://daily.jstor.org/plant-of-the-month-hibiscus/.

Ibhulu

Zukulu, Sinegugu, Tony Dold, Tony Abbott, and others. 2012. *Medicinal and Charm Plants of Pondoland.* Gauteng: South African National Biodiversity Institute.

Iroko

Rashford, John. 2013. "Candomblé's Cosmic Tree and Brazil's Ficus

Species." In *African Ethnobotany in the Americas*, edited by Robert Voeks and John Rashford, 311–33. New York: Springer.

Sodré, Jaime. 1995. *As histórias de lokoirokotempo : a árvore sagrada o Candomblé*. Salvador: Self-published. (Portuguese)

Jackalberry

Fandohan, B., A.E. Assogbadjo, V.K. Salako, P. van Damme, et al. 2012. "Which One Comes First, the Tamarind or the *Macrotermes* Termitarium?"_ Acta Botanica Gallica_ 159 (3): 345–55.

Hubbell, Diana. 2021. "For Enslaved Cooks, Persimmon Beer Combined Ingenuity and Joy." *Atlas Obscura*. November 12, 2021. http://www.atlasobscura.com/articles/michael-twitty-persimmon-beer.

Jatoba

Jansen, Patrick A., Ben T. Hirsch, Willem-Jan Emsens, Veronica Zamora-Gutierrez, et al. 2012. "Thieving Rodents as Substitute Dispersers of Megafaunal Seeds." *Proceedings of the National Academy of Sciences* 109 (31): 12610–15.

Kapok

Hartman, Joseph. 2011. "The Ceiba Tree as a Multivocal Signifier: Afro-Cuban Symbolism, Political Performance, and Urban Space in the Cuban Republic." *Hemisphere* 4 (1): 16.

Tareau, Marc-Alexandre, Alexander Greene, Guillaume Odonne, and Damien Davy. 2022. "*Ceiba Pentandra* (Malvaceae) and Associated Species: Spiritual Keystone Species of the Neotropics." *Botany* 100 (2): 127–40.

Lemon

García-Sánchez, Expiración, Julia María Carabaza Bravo, and J. Esteban Hernández-Bermejo. 2021. *Flora Agrícola y Forestal de Al-Andalus Volumen II: Especies Leñosas*. Madrid: Ministerio de agricultura, alimentación y medio ambiente. (Spanish)

Muthukumaran, Sureshkumar. 2023. *The Tropical Turn: Agricultural Innovation in the Ancient Middle East and the Mediterranean*. Berkeley: University of California Press.

Sonneman, Toby. 2012. *Lemon: A Global History*. London: Reaktion.

Liana

Grossman, Daniel. 2017. "The Strange Case of the Liana Vine and Its Role in Global Warming." *Yale E360,* April 13, 2017. https://e360.yale.edu/features/the-strange-case-of-the-liana-vine-and-its-role-in-global-warming.

Rowe, Nick. 2018. "Lianas." *Current Biology* 28 (6): 249-52.

Mallow

Fuentes Elías, Ismael. 2013. "Vudú y rará en Elena Celestien Vidal: rutas haitianas en el Oriente cubano." *Batey* 4 (4): 56-80.

Millet

Gunderson, Frank D. 2010. *Sukuma Labor Songs from Western Tanzania: We Never Sleep, We Dream of Farming.* Leiden: Brill.

National Research Council. 1996. *Lost Crops of Africa*, vol. 1. Washington, D.C: The National Academies Press.

Natal Cycad

Golding, Janice. 1998. "An Encounter with the Rain Queen's Cycads." *Veld & Flora*, December 1998.

Ndlovu, Siphelele, Terence N. Suinyuy, María A. Pérez-Fernández, and Anathi Magadlela. 2023. "Encephalartos Natalensis, Their Nutrient-Cycling Microbes and Enzymes: A Story of Successful Trade-Offs." Plants 12 (5): 1034. https://doi.org/10.3390/plants12051034.

Zukulu, Sinegugu, Tony Dold, Tony Abbott, et al. 2012. *Medicinal and Charm Plants of Pondoland.* Gauteng: South African National Biodiversity Institute.

Nutmeg

Ghosh, Amitav. 2021. *The Nutmeg's Curse: Parables for a Planet in Crisis.* Chicago: University of Chicago Press.

Keens-Douglas, Richardo. 1992. *The Nutmeg Princess.* Toronto: Annick Press.

Okra

Cabrera, Lydia. 2023. *El Monte: Notes on the Religions, Magic, and Folklore of the Black and Creole People of Cuba.* Translated by David Font-Navarrete. Durham, NC: Duke University Press.

National Research Council. 2006. *Lost Crops of Africa*, vol. 2. Washington, D.C: The National Academies Press.

Onion

Kurlansky, Mark. 2023. "A Brief History of Onions in America: On Ramps, Xonacatl, Skunk Eggs and More." *Literary Hub*, November 9, 2023. https://lithub.com/a-brief-history-of-onions-in-america/.

Orange

Klein, Shana. 2017. "ORANGES FROM HARRIET BEECHER STOWE—MANDARIN, FLA." *Southern Cultures*, Fall 2017. https://www.southerncultures.org/article/oranges-from-harriet-beecher-stowe/.

Palm

Taussig, Michael. 2018. *Palma Africana*. Chicago: University of Chicago Press.

Papaya

VanBuren, Robert, Fanchang Zeng, Cuixia Chen, Jisen Zhang, et al. 2015. "Origin and Domestication of Papaya Yh Chromosome." *Genome Research* 25 (4): 524–33.

Pea

Twitty, Michael W. 2019. "The Cowpea: A Recipe for Resilience." *Emergence Magazine*, October 9, 2019. https://emergencemagazine.org/essay/the-cowpea-a-recipe-for-resilience/.

Mallory, Sarrah, Emily Kamm, Haley Price, and Christina Hourigan. 2022/ "Black-Eyed Pea: Crop, Culture, Class." *Dumbarton Oaks Plant Humanities Lab*. https://lab.plant-humanities.org/black_eyed_peas/.

National Research Council. 2006. *Lost Crops of Africa*, vol. 2. Washington, D.C: The National Academies Press.

Peanut

Johnson-Roehr, S. N. 2022. "Plant of the Month: Peanut." *JSTOR Daily*, May 18, 2022. https://daily.jstor.org/plant-of-the-month-peanut/.

Pear

García-Sánchez, Expiración, Julia María Carabaza Bravo, and J. Esteban Hernández-Bermejo. 2021. *Flora Agrícola y Forestal de Al-Andalus Volumen II: Especies Leñosas*. Madrid: Ministerio de agricultura, alimentación y medio ambiente. (Spanish)

Pine

Fall, Patricia L., Peter J. van Hengstum, Lisa Lavold-Foote, Jeffrey P. Donnelly, et al. 2021. "Human Arrival and Landscape Dynamics in the Northern Bahamas." *Proceedings of the National Academy of Sciences* 118 (10).

Plantain

Scafe-Smith, Akil. 2020. "Going Banana, Becoming Plantain." *The Funambulist*, August 27, 2020.

Wilks, Ivor. 2005. "The Forest and the Twis." *Journal des africanistes*, no. 75-1 (September): 19-75.

Pumpkin

Adeyemi, Sola. 2012. "Performing Myths, Ritualising Modernity: Dancing for Nomkhubulwana and the Reinvention of Zulu Tradition." In *A Gazelle of the Savannah: Sunday Ododo and the Framing of Techno-Cultural Performance in Nigeria*, edited by Osakue S. Omoera, Sola Adeyemi, and Benedict Bineba, 435-45. Rochester, UK: Alpha Crownes.

Douglass, Frederick. 1849. "Pumpkins." *The North Star (Rochester, N.Y.)*, October 19, 1849.

Ott, Cindy. 2012. *Pumpkin: The Curious History of an American Icon*. Washington: University of Washington Press.

Raspberry

Hedrick, U. P. 1925. *The Small Fruits of New York*. Albany: J. B. Lyon.

Treat, James. 2011. "Kvco-Hvse, 'Blackberry Month.'" *The Native Times*, June 5, 2011. https://nativetimes.com/index.php?option=com_content&view=article&id=5496.

Rose

Hayes, Joe. 2010. *Dance, Nana, Dance / Baila, Nana, Baila. Cuban Folktales in English and Spanish*. El Paso, TX: Cinco Puntos Press.

Horwood, Catherine. 2018. *Rose*. London: Reaktion.

García-Sánchez, Expiración, Julia María Carabaza Bravo, and J. Esteban Hernández-Bermejo. 2021. *Flora Agrícola y Forestal de Al-Andalus Volumen II: Especies Leñosas*. Madrid: Ministerio de agricultura, alimentación y medio ambiente. (Spanish)

Rubber Tree

Whaley, W. Gordon. 1948. "Rubber: The Primary Sources for American Production." *Economic Botany* 2 (2): 198–216.

Safu

Maneniang, Mubima. 1999. *The Lianja Epic.* Nairobi: East African Educational Publishers.

National Research Council. 2008. *Lost Crops of Africa*, vol. 3. Washington, D.C: The National Academies Press.

Sarsaparilla

Miller, Allison. 2021. "Plant of the Month: Sarsaparilla." *JSTOR Daily*, June 16, 2021. https://daily.jstor.org/plant-of-the-month-sarsaparilla/.

Winterbottom, Anna E. 2015. "Of the China Root: A Case Study of the Early Modern Circulation of Materia Medica." *Social History of Medicine* 28 (1): 22–44.

Shea

Elias, Marlène, and Judith Carney. 2007. "African Shea Butter: A Feminized Subsidy from Nature." *Africa* 77 (1): 37–62.

National Research Council. 2006. *Lost Crops of Africa*, vol. 2. Washington, D.C: The National Academies Press.

Sorghum

National Research Council. 1996. *Lost Crops of Africa*, vol. 1. Washington, D.C: The National Academies Press.

Soursop

Carlson, Betsy and Bill Keegan. 2005. "Talking Taíno: If You Like Pina Coladas..." *Times of the Islands,* Summer 2005.

Star Apple

Lichtveld, Ursy M., and Jan Voorhoeve. 1975. *Creole Drum: An Anthology of Creole Literature in Surinam.* Translated by Vernie A. February. New Haven: Yale University Press.

Walcott, Derek. 1978. "The Star-Apple Kingdom." *The American Poetry Review* 7 (3): 3–6.

Sugarcane

Bosma, Ulbe. 2023. *The World of Sugar: How the Sweet Stuff*

Transformed Our Politics, Health, and Environment over 2,000 Years. Cambridge, MA: Belknap.

Mintz, Sidney. 1986. *Sweetness and Power: the Place of Sugar in Modern History.* New York: Penguin.

Pérez, Elizabeth. 2015. "Crystallizing Subjectivities in the African Diaspora: Sugar, Honey, and the Gods of Afro-Cuban Lucumí." In *Religion, Food, and Eating in North America*, 175-94. New York: Columbia University Press.

Tamarind

Fandohan, B., A.E. Assogbadjo, V.K. Salako, P. van Damme, and B. Sinsin. 2012. "Which One Comes First, the Tamarind or the Macrotermes Termitarium?" *Acta Botanica Gallica* 159 (3): 345-55.

Niane, Djibril Tamsir. 2006. *Sundiata: An Epic of Old Mali.* Revised Edition. London: Pearson Longman.

Taro

van Andel, Tinde R., Amber van der Velden, and Minke Reijers. 2016. "The 'Botanical Gardens of the Dispossessed' Revisited: Richness and Significance of Old World Crops Grown by Suriname Maroons." *Genetic Resources and Crop Evolution* 63 (4): 695-710.

Trumpet Tree

Pelton, John. 1964. "A Survey of the Ecology of *Tecoma Stans.*" *Butler University Botanical Studies* 14 (2): 53-88.

Umabophe

Koopman, A. 2013. "The Interface between Magic, Plants and Language." *Southern African Humanities* 25: 87-103.

Zukulu, Sinegugu, Tony Dold, Tony Abbott, et al. 2012. *Medicinal and Charm Plants of Pondoland.* Gauteng: South African National Biodiversity Institute.

Water Cabbage

Ajao, Abdulwakeel A., Yusuf Ola Mukaila, and Saheed Sabiu. 2022. "Wandering through Southwestern Nigeria: An Inventory of Yoruba Useful Angiosperm Plants." *Heliyon* 8 (1).

Watermelon

Mitchell, Shane. 2023. "The Wounded Fruit." *The Bitter Southerner*, August 23, 2023. https://bittersoutherner.com/feature/2023/watermelon-the-wounded-fruit-shane-mitchell.

Paris, Harry S. 2023. "Origin of the Dessert Watermelon." In *The Watermelon Genome*, edited by Sudip Kr. Dutta, Padma Nimmakayala, and Umesh K. Reddy, 1–16. New York: Springer.

Yam

Wynter, Sylvia. 1971. "Novel and History, Plot and Plantation." *Savacou* 5 (1): 95–102.

Yerba Mate

Mertehikian, Lucas. 2023. "Plant of the Month: Yerba Mate." *JSTOR Daily.* January 5, 2023. https://daily.jstor.org/plant-of-the-month-yerba-mate/.

Staffolani, Claudio, Lucio Alcaíno, Silvia Tessio Conca, and Natalia Ojeda. 2021. "La ronda del mate en Paraná, un espacio territorial para repensar el patrimonio cultural inmaterial" *Scientia Interfluvius* 12. (Spanish and English)

ABOUT THE AUTHOR

Natty Mark Samuels, dubbed "Oxford's botanical folklorist" by *OX Magazine*, travels to community projects, carnivals, and botanical gardens throughout the UK telling the stories and singing the songs of African and Caribbean flora. In 2009, seeing that none of Oxford's universities offered undergraduate tuition in African Studies, Samuels founded the African School, where he teaches classes on African folklore, history, and art.